"Dustin Benge provides us with an absolute gem—a beautiful condensation of all that is good about the local church. With ease of prose, Benge introduces us to the multicolored facets of what the church is and how she functions to grow us into the people of God. A marvelous read."

Derek W. H. Thomas, Senior Minister, First Presbyterian Church, Columbia, South Carolina; Teaching Fellow, Ligonier Ministries; Chancellor's Professor, Reformed Theological Seminary

"The true and faithful church is the beautiful bride of Christ. In the experience of reading this refreshing treatment, all who love the church will rejoice in the realization of her beauty. Many people are concerned about how the world views the church. The world will never have the right perspective until the church itself sees her beauty. Surely this is what the apostle Paul meant when he said in 2 Corinthians 11:2 that he desired to present the church as a chaste virgin to Christ. This book is a much-needed gift to the people of God."

John MacArthur, Pastor, Grace Community Church, Sun Valley, California; Chancellor, The Master's University and Seminary

"This is a rich reflection upon the nature of the church. Benge rightly shows us the way the church is viewed from heaven and from the eschaton. If we could only grasp the glorious beauty of the church in the light of these two perspectives, the negativity that too often crosses our lips and permeates our minds about the triune God's beloved would be replaced with wonder and awe. Warmly recommended."

Michael A. G. Haykin, Chair and Professor of Church History, The Southern Baptist Theological Seminary

"A little more than a decade ago I said I'd never seen such a profound unity in the church. What has happened? Leadership failures, unresolved conflicts, high-profile apostasies, political division, social upheaval, a global pandemic, theological controversy, and more. Is greater church unity possible again? Of course it is, but any movement toward unity must be dependent on the Holy Spirit and based on God's truth. May the Lord use *The Loveliest Place*, in which Dustin Benge faithfully sets forth the glories of God's truth about the church, to rebuild our unity."

Donald S. Whitney, Professor of Biblical Spirituality and Associate Dean, The Southern Baptist Theological Seminary

"Do you consider the church to be lovely? Jesus does. He looks at his blood-bought bride with deep delight and desires that we do the same. In *The Loveliest Place*, Dustin Benge introduces us afresh to the church in a way that rekindles affection and renews commitment. Many books tell us about the church, but few help us love the church. This important work refreshes the soul and inspires worship."

Garrett Kell, Lead Pastor, Del Ray Baptist Church, Alexandria, Virginia

"Beholding the true beauty of the church can often be a challenge because many times she is torn asunder by various scandals and divisions. Dustin Benge nevertheless calls us to view the church from the divine perspective as the chosen bride of Christ. Only through this corrective lens can we recognize how precious she is in the sight of our triune God. May God give us eyes to see her radiant glory as she is clothed with the glistening garments of Christ."

Steven J. Lawson, President, OnePassion Ministries; Professor of Preaching, The Master's Seminary; Teaching Fellow, Ligonier Ministries

THE LOVELIEST PLACE

Union

A book series edited by Michael Reeves

Rejoice and Tremble: The Surprising Good News of the Fear of the Lord, Michael Reeves (2021)

What Does It Mean to Fear the Lord?, Michael Reeves (2021, concise version of *Rejoice and Tremble*)

Deeper: Real Change for Real Sinners, Dane C. Ortlund (2021)

How Does God Change Us?, Dane C. Ortlund (2021, concise version of *Deeper*)

The Loveliest Place: The Beauty and Glory of the Church, Dustin Benge (2022)

Why Should We Love the Local Church?, Dustin Benge (2022, concise version of *The Loveliest Place*)

THE LOVELIEST PLACE

The Beauty and Glory of the Church

DUSTIN BENGE

WHEATON, ILLINOIS

The Loveliest Place: The Beauty and Glory of the Church
Copyright © 2022 by Dustin Benge
Published by Crossway
        1300 Crescent Street
        Wheaton, Illinois 60187

Cover design: Jordan Singer
Cover image: "New England Scenery" (1839) by Thomas Cole (Wikimedia commons)
First printing 2022
Printed in the United States of America

Hardcover ISBN: 978-1-4335-7494-8
ePub ISBN: 978-1-4335-7497-9
PDF ISBN: 978-1-4335-7495-5
Mobipocket ISBN: 978-1-4335-7496-2

Library of Congress Cataloging-in-Publication Data
Names: Benge, Dustin W., author.
Title: The loveliest place : the beauty and glory of the church / Dustin Benge.
Description: Wheaton, Illinois : Crossway, [2022] | Series: Union | Includes bibliographical references and index.
Identifiers: LCCN 2021021539 (print) | LCCN 2021021540 (ebook) | ISBN 9781433574948 (hardcover) | ISBN 9781433574955 (epdf) | ISBN 9781433574962 (mobipocket) | ISBN 9781433574979 (epub)
Subjects: LCSH: Church.
Classification: LCC BV600.3 .B4625 2022 (print) | LCC BV600.3 (ebook) | DDC 262—dc23
LC record available at https://lccn.loc.gov/2021021539
LC ebook record available at https://lccn.loc.gov/2021021540

Crossway is a publishing ministry of Good News Publishers.

V P   31   30   29   28   27   26   25   24   23   22
15   14   13   12   11   10   9   8   7   6   5   4   3   2   1

To Nate Pickowicz,
my friend, brother,
and co-laborer in the gospel

Contents

Series Preface   *11*

Introduction   *13*

1   You Are Beautiful   *17*

2   The Household of God   *29*

3   Our Father and Friend   *39*

4   Our Savior and Head   *49*

5   Our Helper and Beautifier   *61*

6   A Pillar and Buttress of Truth   *75*

7   In Spirit and Truth   *87*

8   Shepherding the Flock   *97*

9   Feeding the Flock   *111*

10   Good News   *121*

11   In Remembrance   *131*

12   Walking Worthy   *143*

13   Blessed Persecution   *155*

14   We Are One   *169*

Epilogue *181*

General Index *185*

Scripture Index *191*

Series Preface

OUR INNER CONVICTIONS AND VALUES shape our lives and our ministries. And at Union—the cooperative ministries of Union School of Theology, Union Publishing, Union Research, and Union Mission (visit www.theolo.gy)—we long to grow and support men and women who will delight in God, grow in Christ, serve the church, and bless the world. This Union series of books is an attempt to express and share those values.

They are values that flow from the beauty and grace of God. The living God is so glorious and kind, he cannot be known without being adored. Those who truly know him will love him, and without that heartfelt delight in God, we are nothing but hollow hypocrites. That adoration of God necessarily works itself out in a desire to grow in Christlikeness. It also fuels a love for Christ's precious bride, the church, and a desire humbly to serve—rather than use—her. And, lastly, loving God brings us to share his concerns, especially to see his life-giving glory fill the earth.

Each exploration of a subject in the Union series will appear in two versions: a full volume and a concise one. The idea is that church leaders can read the full treatment, such as this one, and so delve into each topic while making the more accessible concise version widely available to their congregations.

My hope and prayer is that these books will bless you and your church as you develop a deeper delight in God that overflows in joyful integrity, humility, Christlikeness, love for the church, and a passion to make disciples of all nations.

Michael Reeves
SERIES EDITOR

Introduction

WE ALL HAVE SPECIAL PLACES we visit, either in person or in memory. For me, one of those treasured places is the farm of my grandparents. Running through freshly plowed fields, climbing majestic oaks, and sitting at the table of my grandmother's cooking—there's no place I would rather be. This place evokes a sense of joy, comfort, and home.

When we think of the church, does it arouse similar deep affection? Can we say the church is one of those unique places that conjures a sincere sense of longing, delight, and home?

Nineteenth-century preacher Charles Haddon Spurgeon captures the admiration all true believers should have for the church in his depiction of her as "the dearest place on earth."[1] Chosen by God the Father, purchased by Christ the Son, and empowered by the Holy Spirit, the church should be cherished and recognized as "dear" by all who call her home. *Dear* is not a word we often hear in our modern context, but its definition amply conveys what Spurgeon is communicating to all believers concerning the church. It suggests deep

---

1   Charles H. Spurgeon, "The Best Donation" (exposition, April 5, 1891), in *The Metropolitan Tabernacle Pulpit: Containing Sermons Preached and Revised*, vol. 37 (Pasadena, TX: Pilgrim, 1975), 633.

affection. You may refer to someone as a "dear friend," meaning that you warmly esteem that person and consider him or her a particular treasure in your life. By calling Christ's church "dear," Spurgeon says there is nothing in this present life that we should find more precious to our hearts, for this is how God himself perceives her. Spurgeon continues, "Nothing in the world is dearer to God's heart than his church; therefore, being his, let us also belong to it, that by our prayers, our gifts, and our labours, we may support and strengthen it."[2]

It's all too easy to allow our warmth toward the church to slip away, as we grow cold and apathetic. Honestly, the church can often be a difficult place to think of as dear or lovely. However, when we shift our perspective from our puny self-interest, which often fuels our disgruntlement toward the church, she not only becomes precious to us but also becomes a treasure of eternal joy, beauty, and love.

This book is about the beauty and loveliness of the church. It's for all those who sometimes struggle to see those qualities in her. If you tirelessly serve within her ministries while dismayed by her apparent failures, or have rare, unsustainable glimpses of her beauty, this book is for you. The singular goal is to awaken your affections. Not affections for form, methodology, structure, organization, or programs, but affections for *who* she is and *why* she exists.

You might ask, why is such a book needed?

Every generation faces the seemingly insurmountable challenge of biblically defining the church because our modern definitions never seem to shift from functionality and success to beauty and loveliness.

The church is the assembly of the redeemed. Those who have been called by God the Father to salvation through Christ the Son

2 Spurgeon, "The Best Donation," 633, 635.

make up her assembly (John 6:37). The apostle Peter describes her as being composed of those called "out of darkness into his marvelous light" (1 Pet. 2:9). The church, then, is the corporate gathering of the redeemed citizens of heaven, who have been transmitted from the dominion of darkness into the kingdom of Christ through his shed blood, glorious resurrection, exalted ascension, and present intercession (Col. 1:13). This biblical understanding sets the trajectory of every believer's life, calling, and service in ministry, as well as our relationship with the whole world.

While the church has a clear command, purpose, and mission, those do not define *who* the church is. There's a deeper and more satisfying well from which to drink that, once realized, fuels such service and mission. Therefore, to capture her beauty and loveliness, the church must be defined not by *what* we do but by *who* we are.

There is no more robust and doxological foundation upon which we can build a definition of the church than the eternal work of the Father, Son, and Holy Spirit. In the words of eighteenth-century New England pastor-theologian Jonathan Edwards, the whole world was created so that "the eternal Son of God might obtain a spouse."[3] The church is not a Trinitarian afterthought in response to man's fall in the garden—quite the contrary. The church is the focused domain where all God's presence, promises, and purposes are unveiled and eternally realized.

The church's beauty and loveliness are most vividly portrayed in the brilliant metaphor of her as the "bride of Christ." In his instructions to husbands regarding the love they should have for their wives, the

3 Jonathan Edwards, "The Church's Marriage to Her Sons, and to Her God," in *Sermons and Discourses, 1743–1758*, ed. Wilson H. Kimnach, vol. 25 of *The Works of Jonathan Edwards* (New Haven, CT: Yale University Press, 2006), 187.

apostle Paul writes, "Love your wives, as Christ loved the church and gave himself up for her" (Eph. 5:25). This stunning bride is arrayed in snow-white garments washed in the redeeming blood of Christ (Rev. 7:14), and beholding her beauty, a vast multitude cries out,

> The marriage of the Lamb has come,
> and his Bride has made herself ready. (Rev. 19:7)

God gives the church to Christ as his bride, Edwards says, "so that the mutual joys between this bride and bridegroom are the end of the creation."[4]

As the creation of God, the church is a means through which the Father delights in Christ as the object of his eternal love and divine happiness. The church's life is beautifully framed by her position as the reward to Christ for his suffering on the cross, thus making Christ a worthy groom for his bride. This glorious union between Christ and his church will never be severed. The two, joined together by God, are eternally satisfied in one another as they bask in the glory, majesty, and holiness of God.

This book has one aim: to set before you a thoroughly biblical portrait of the church that derives its life from the sweet fellowship of the Father, Son, and Spirit, creating a community of love, worship, fellowship, and mission, all animated by the gospel and empowered by the word of God.

By beholding such radiant beauty and loveliness, may we lift our collective and worshipful cry, "Indeed, the church is the loveliest place on earth."

---

4 Jonathan Edwards, *Writings on the Trinity, Grace, and Faith*, ed. Sang Hyun Lee, vol. 21 of *The Works of Jonathan Edwards* (New Haven, CT: Yale University Press, 2003), 142.

1

You Are Beautiful

Behold, you are beautiful, my love;
behold, you are beautiful.

SONG OF SOLOMON 1:15

THE CHURCH IS BEAUTIFUL.

Beautiful is not a phrase we often associate with the church. Words like *organization, mission, vision,* and even *body* come to mind, but not *beautiful.*

We like helpful organizational charts that describe the purpose and function of the church. We want to place her members in properly assigned roles and duties. We underscore the qualifications and responsibilities of church leaders. We emphasize the church's theology and mission among the nations. We even pinpoint and seem to critique her problems and failures endlessly. While all of these diminutive details may be necessary for fulfilling her divine task on earth, there's a cumulative danger of consigning the church to mere administrative categories that are indistinguishable from our neighborhood civic club.

We consider what the church can give us and do for us, how she can serve us, and even what's in it for us, but rarely do we enjoy the eye-opening and soul-stirring truth that she is beautiful and lovely in just *being* who she is.

The church has played a central role in many of our lives. She has nurtured in times of grief, shepherded in valleys of despair, and instructed in seasons of growth. We love her people. We love her ministries. We love her worship. We love her teaching. We love her comfort.

Do we love her?

Does your heart swell with deep and abiding affection at the mention of her name and the prospect of dwelling in the company of her people? Can we say of her, as her bridegroom does,

> You are beautiful, my love;
>> behold, you are beautiful (Song 1:15)?

Admired by Christ

Reflecting on Song of Solomon 1:15, John Gill, an eighteenth-century English Baptist pastor, wrote, "These are the words of Christ, commending the beauty of the church, expressing his great affection for her, and his high esteem of her; of her fairness and beauty."[1] Gill interprets Song of Solomon as an intense allegorical portrayal of the love, union, and communion that exists between Jesus Christ and his bride, the church. In chapter 1, the bridegroom fixes his eternal attention upon the bride and identifies her as "beautiful."

What must it be like to be admired by the sinless Son of God? Rather than admire her, we imagine he would identify her failures, her shortcomings, and the loathsome sin that so often spoils her gar-

---

1   John Gill, *An Exposition of the Book of Solomon's Song* (London: William Hill Collingridge, 1854), 57.

ments. Instead, through the eyes of a bridegroom transfixed upon his bride, Christ invites our gaze with the attention-grabbing, "Behold!" Her beauty commands awe, wonder, and astonishment.

More profound amazement is ours when we consider that the church is composed of sinners. Albeit forgiven, still sinners. In her own eyes, the church is full of spots and blemishes and is, in fact, sometimes disgusting to behold. Paul says that only at the end of the age will the church be presented to Christ "in splendor, without spot or wrinkle or any such thing" (Eph. 5:27). Yet Christ draws our attention to his bride here and now, not for veneration, but that we may be astonished and lost in the wonder of his love and sacrifice on her behalf.

The church is beautiful because the lens through which Christ regards her is his cross—the focal point of blood, righteousness, forgiveness, union, justification, regeneration, and grace. His cross makes her beautiful. His perfection makes her beautiful. It is his sacrificial, substitutionary, sinless blood that washes her garments as white as snow. The cross of Christ makes her beautiful not only inwardly by justification but also outwardly through sanctification. From giving second birth to final glory, the righteousness of Christ creates a beautiful church.

His perfect righteousness fashions a loveliness so shocking and captivating that in the same sentence he repeats his admiration twice:

Behold you are beautiful . . . ;
    behold, you are beautiful. (Song 1:15)

Then with pictorial detail, the bridegroom begins to characterize the beauty of his bride. Ask any adoring husband to attempt such an explanation of his bride, and he will fail at words. "Your eyes are doves" (Song 1:15). Doves mate for life and are often represented in weddings because they symbolize a lifetime of love. The bond is so strong that it can extend, for a time, beyond death as they watch over their mates, trying to care for them, and returning again and again to the place of their death. The ever-watchful dove looks only to its mate and has no eyes for another.

Christ has eyes only for his church. Believers, saved by grace through faith, are espoused exclusively to him. His righteousness, pardon, forgiveness, love, care, provision, eternal life—these are only for her. His singular eye is upon her at all times. He exclaims, "You have captivated my heart with one glance of your eyes" (Song 4:9). There's never a time when Christ doesn't love her. There's never a time when he doesn't extend his whole heart to her. There's never a time his heart isn't captivated by her.

If, with Gill, we were to interpret Solomon's words as emblematic of Christ and his church, in that context, listen to what he would be saying to her:

> Behold, you are beautiful, my love,
>   behold, you are beautiful!
> Your eyes are doves
>   behind your veil.
> Your hair is like a flock of goats
>   leaping down the slopes of Gilead.
> Your teeth are like a flock of shorn ewes
>   that have come up from the washing,
> all of which bear twins,
>   and not one among them has lost its young.
> Your lips are like a scarlet thread,
>   and your mouth is lovely.
> Your cheeks are like halves of a pomegranate
>   behind your veil.

Your neck is like the tower of David,
    built in rows of stone;
on it hang a thousand shields,
    all of them shields of warriors.
Your two breasts are like two fawns,
    twins of a gazelle,
    that graze among the lilies.
Until the day breathes
    and the shadows flee,
I will go away to the mountain of myrrh
    and the hill of frankincense.
You are altogether beautiful, my love;
    there is no flaw in you. (Song 4:1–7)

The bridegroom employs rich creation language here to distinguish the beauty and loveliness of his bride. Though it is not quite how we might describe the attention of our love, the ancient world would immediately recognize wonder in such imaginative beauty. Leaping goats, freshly washed ewes, ruby red pomegranates, shielded stone towers, lilies of the field, leaping gazelles, and rare spices dripping from the mountains—this lovely bride is arrayed in the cloak of God's creation. She is more beautiful than any composition of man—the *Mona Lisa*, the Riviera at sunset, or the New York skyline glittering at night. She resembles all that God said was good in his perfect creation. She is Christ's delight, having been redeemed, washed in his blood, and sanctified by his Spirit, and he calls her (us) "my love."

Reflected Beauty

At this point, it's necessary to clarify that the beauty of the church is not a type of romantic or inherently attractive beauty that causes one to blush. The church would never adorn the cover of a magazine because she is beautiful.

The beauty of the church is the reflection of another—God. David says,

> One thing have I asked of the LORD,
>   that will I seek after:
> that I may dwell in the house of the LORD
>   all the days of my life,
> to gaze upon the *beauty* of the LORD
>   and to inquire in his temple. (Ps. 27:4)

As if scrutinizing every facet of a brilliantly cut diamond, David confesses that he could spend all the days of his life gazing upon the beauty of the Lord. Asaph joins David in his admiration of God's perfect beauty:

> Out of Zion, the perfection of beauty,
>   God shines forth. (Ps. 50:2)

There are no satisfactory words to define or portray the beauty of God. The prophet Isaiah foretells a day when the Lord of hosts "will be a crown of glory" and "a diadem of beauty" to his people (Isa. 28:5). To come face-to-face with God's transcendent beauty is to ascend to the peak of our deepest longing and the fulfillment of our greatest desires.

God's beauty and loveliness shine forth most radiantly through the biblical concept of glory. Moses experienced this glory when God passed by him, revealing only the afterglow of his grandeur (Ex. 33:12–23). When God's glory engulfed the temple, the priests were unable to perform their service of worship (2 Chron. 5:14). Isaiah found himself facedown in the dirt when he witnessed God's glory emanating from his eternal throne (Isa. 6:1–5). Peter, James, and John became like dead men as God's glory sparkled in their eyes when Christ transfigured before them (Matt. 17:1–8). In our fallen state, to behold God's refulgent glory would cause us to fall dead in wonder, love, and praise.

Jonathan Edwards, reflecting on God's glory and beauty, wrote,

> For as God is infinitely the greatest Being, so he is allowed to be infinitely the most beautiful and excellent: and all the beauty to be found throughout the whole creation is but the reflection of the diffused beams of that Being who hath an infinite fullness of brightness and glory; God . . . is the foundation and fountain of all being and all beauty.[2]

Like a prism that splits light into a myriad of colors, everything in God's creation is a mere reflection of the one radiant beam of glory emanating from God's inherent perfection and holiness. God's beauty isn't exhibited in his flawless skin tone, waving hair, perfectly set eyes, or impeccably symmetrical nose, for he has none of the physical attributes that we often classify as beautiful. Edwards regards the beauty of God as the differentiating feature of God himself: "God is God, and is distinguished from all other beings, and exalted above 'em, chiefly by his divine beauty, which is infinitely diverse from all other beauty."[3] God's beauty emanates directly from his being. All other creatures receive their beauty from outside sources. God is not dependent upon other things or persons to make him beautiful, for he is "beauty

---

2 Jonathan Edwards, *The Nature of True Virtue: A Jonathan Edwards Reader*, ed. John E. Smith, Harry S. Stout, and Kenneth P. Minkema (London: Yale University Press, 1995), 252–53.

3 Jonathan Edwards, *Religious Affections*, ed. John E. Smith, vol. 2 of *The Works of Jonathan Edwards* (New Haven, CT: Yale University Press, 1959), 298.

within himself."[4] Beauty is one of the defining characteristics of God's uniqueness and transcendence, for he is its foundation and fountain.

The supreme expression of God's beauty is his Son, Jesus Christ, who himself is the image and radiance of his Father. Paul affirms Jesus as "the image of God" (2 Cor. 4:4). That is, to see Jesus is to see God, to hear Jesus is to hear God, to know Jesus is to know God. Again, in Colossians 1:15, Paul classifies Jesus as "the image of the invisible God." The writer of Hebrews echoes the same language: "He [Jesus] is the radiance of the glory of God and the exact imprint of his nature" (Heb. 1:3). As glory is a defining characteristic of God's nature, the beauty that shines forth from God also shines forth from Jesus, for Jesus is the visible incarnation of God's radiant glory.

Edwards identifies Christ as the end for which God created the world and how God most vividly expresses his beautiful love to sinful creatures. The expression of that love is selecting a bride for Christ that she too might beam with the same beauty as her bridegroom. Edwards reflects, "Christ is divine wisdom, so that the world is made to gratify divine love as exercised by Christ, or to gratify the love that is in Christ's heart, or to provide a spouse for Christ—those creatures which wisdom chooses for the object of divine love as Christ's elect spouse."[5] To express his infinite love for Christ, God gives him a spouse, the church. In a sermon on Revelation 22 preached in May 1741, Edwards continues this meditation:

> Christ obtaining this spouse is the great end of all the great things that have been done from the beginning of the world; it was that

4 Roland André Delattre, *Beauty and Sensibility in the Thought of Jonathan Edwards: An Essay in Aesthetics and Theological Ethics* (New Haven, CT: Yale University Press, 1968), 152.
5 Jonathan Edwards, *Writings on the Trinity, Grace, and Faith*, ed. Sang Hyun Lee, vol. 21 of *The Works of Jonathan Edwards* (New Haven, CT: Yale University Press, 2003), 142.

the son of God might obtain his chosen spouse that the world was created . . . and that he came into the world . . . and when this end shall be fully obtained, the world will come to an end.[6]

The church is a gift from God to his Son "so that the mutual joys between this bride and bridegroom are the end of creation."[7] Therefore, as the Son is a reflection of his Father, the church, as his eternal bride, is a reflection of the Son.

When Christ lovingly looks upon his bride and exclaims that she is "beautiful," he beholds the reflection of the everlasting glory and infinite love of his Father, who is the primary fountain from which all true beauty flows. Since Christ's ascension to the right hand of the majesty on high, there is now no more brilliant exemplification of God's perfect beauty in this world than his church.

God could have chosen to make his beauty known exclusively through breathtaking landscapes, undulating oceans, and sublime sunsets. Instead, he has decided to display his radiance within the hearts of the crown of his creation, humanity. As a result, he has chosen a people, his church, to reflect his glory to the world.

The church is beautiful because God is beautiful.

The Bride's Affection

Not only does Christ lavish his affection upon the church as the object of his joyful love, but the church also reveres her bridegroom with

6 Jonathan Edwards, unpublished sermon on Revelation 22:16–17 (May 1741), accessed from the Jonathan Edwards Center at Yale University, 2011, L. 3v. See also Rhys S. Bezzant, *Jonathan Edwards and the Church* (New York: Oxford University Press, 2014), 59.
7 Jonathan Edwards, "Miscellanies," 271, in *The Miscellanies, Entry Nos. a–z, aa–zz, 1–500*, ed. Thomas A. Schafer, vol. 13 of *The Works of Jonathan Edwards* (New Haven, CT: Yale University Press, 1994), 374.

the same unshakable devotion. She describes him as "distinguished among ten thousand" (Song 5:10), having "lips . . . dripping liquid myrrh" (v. 13), "arms . . . set with jewels" (v. 14), "legs . . . set on bases of gold" (v. 15), and "altogether desirable" (v. 16).

Of all who might arrest her attention, Jesus Christ is better than all the rest because he has purchased the church with his blood (Acts 20:28). Christ is beautiful to the church because he rescued her from her enemies and set her in heavenly places (Eph. 2:6). Christ is beautiful to the church because he freely offered his life as payment for a debt she owed (John 10:11). Christ is beautiful to the church because he satisfied God's wrath against her sin and victoriously conquered death (Rom. 3:24–25). Christ is her Savior. Christ is her Redeemer. Christ is her beauty.

Wilhelmus à Brakel, a seventeenth-century Dutch theologian, defines the affection the church has for Christ as one of familiar discourse:

> The soul who thus beholds Jesus, the heart going out in love towards Him, will share with her beloved the frame of her heart, her love, and her grief for not loving him more. She will bring all her needs to him, reveal her desires to him, make supplication to him, plead affectionately with him, and beg of him sweetly for the fulfillment of her desire.[8]

The deep mutual affection shared between two people creates a personal vocabulary that no one else quite understands. Standing across a crowded room from your spouse, for instance, doesn't break the cord of love reciprocally shared. When your eyes meet, the unspoken

---

8 Wilhelmus à Brakel, *The Christian's Reasonable Service*, vol. 2 (Grand Rapids, MI: Reformation Heritage, 2015), 95.

language of love bridges all chasms, and you immediately understand one another. Through God's revealed word to us in Scripture, there exists between Christ and his church a sweet familiar interchange.

> She listens to what Jesus has to say to her, turns herself to his Word, deeming it to be the voice of her beloved. This is particularly true when with clarity, power, and sweetness he impresses a text of Scripture upon her heart, causing her to speak to him in return, giving expression to all the questions generated by her love, which in turn causes Jesus to reply to her. In doing so the soul will lose and forget herself, and it will grieve her if this dialogue is broken off, or if her body is too weak to endure the intensity of her desires as well as the kisses and influences of his love.[9]

Reserved only for the bridegroom and his beloved bride, this intimate dialogue is foreign to the rest of the world as it reveals a complete dependence upon him for all things. "In love she leans upon him, entrusting to him her soul, her body, and whatever she may encounter," à Brakel writes.[10]

Paul describes this dependence as characteristic of the church in Ephesians 4:15–16: "Speaking the truth in love, we are to grow up in every way into him who is the head, into Christ, from whom the whole body, joined and held together by every joint with which it is equipped, when each part is working properly, makes the body grow so that it builds itself up in love." God's great desire for his church is that every believer, without exception, will "grow up in every way into him who is the head into Christ." As we learn to become increasingly dependent upon Christ for all things, God is continually fashioning

9 À Brakel, *The Christian's Reasonable Service*, 95.
10 À Brakel, *The Christian's Reasonable Service*, 95.

the church to mirror the image of Christ. In essence, the church in the world is the beauty of Christ in the world.

We began with the phrase "the church is beautiful." Not that she is beautiful of her own accord or even increasingly beautiful because of her good works, but that she has been made beautiful by the redeeming and propitiatory blood of Christ. Both inwardly and outwardly, the beauty of the church is derived from God through Christ. God has chosen to display his perfect beauty in his beloved bride by giving her to Christ as a majestic reward for his suffering. As a result, the church is the brilliant reflection of God's beauty and loveliness through Christ to the world.

If we accurately grasped the church's beauty and loveliness in all its glorious richness, how dramatically our lives would more appropriately reflect God's plan and purpose. How quickly we would reject petty squabbles that mar our snow-white garments. How lovingly we would serve one another by following the self-denying footsteps of our bridegroom.

"Behold, you are beautiful!" Beholding the church's beauty changes everything.

2

The Household of God

I will be glory in her midst.

ZECHARIAH 2:5

I REMEMBER, AS A BOY, being forbidden from running in the sanctuary of our church. The moment I thought no one was watching, my mom or grandmother would remind me that this was "God's house, and you don't run in God's house."

We don't often think of God having a home, and if we do, our first thoughts turn to heaven. But Scripture repeatedly reminds us that God always dwells among his people.

The Old Testament is full of illustrations of God residing in the center of his people—walking with Adam in the cool of the garden (Gen. 3:8), appearing to Moses in the bush that wasn't consumed (Ex. 3:2), guiding his people through the wilderness by the pillars of cloud by day and of fire by night (Ex. 13:21–22), filling the tabernacle and temple with his shekinah glory (Ex. 40:34–38; Ezek. 43:4). It's impossible to read the history of Israel and not recognize God dwelling in the midst of his people.

When we come to the New Testament, there's no more extraordinary demonstration of God's desire to make his home at the very center of his people than in the incarnation of his only begotten Son, Jesus Christ. John reminds us that "the Word became flesh and dwelt among us" (John 1:14). God's dwelling among Israel was in forms, shadows, and objects. But the condescension of Christ was the light to which all old anthropomorphisms of God pointed. In Christ, God completely bridged the gap between his infinite holiness and man's sinfulness by coming all the way to us. In Christ, God set up his eternal home among his redeemed people.

God's dwelling at the heartbeat of the church has a sovereign uniqueness. While we affirm God's omnipresence among every crevice of the cosmos, Scripture is clear that he resides explicitly in a distinctive and familial way among his people. God dwells in heaven in the sense that his glory, majesty, and holiness are on display there in particular richness. Yet he also assures his people that he will "be glory in [their] midst" (Zech. 2:5).

Moved by his inexhaustible love for the church before the foundation of the world, God resides in her midst with "every spiritual blessing in the heavenly places" (Eph. 1:3), so that even now those who are part of his family on earth are "seated . . . with him in the heavenly places in Christ Jesus" (Eph. 2:6).

God's Family

Defining the church in institutional terms is futile, for the church belongs exclusively to God. In 1 Timothy 3:15, Paul explains to his young son in the faith that he is offering instructions in godliness so that Timothy may know how "to behave in the *household of God*, which is the church of the living God."

The word "household" elicits a metaphor not of a building or structure but of a family—those within the same house. In Acts 16:15, the same analogy describes those within Lydia's household, or family, who became believers. In Matthew 12:46–50, Jesus employs the same family language to designate those who accomplish the will of God:

> While he was still speaking to the people, behold, his mother and his brothers stood outside, asking to speak to him. But he replied to the man who told him, "Who is my mother, and who are my brothers?" And stretching out his hand toward his disciples, he said, "Here are my mother and my brothers! For whoever does the will of my Father in heaven is my brother and sister and mother."

We are brothers and sisters to Christ through our second birth into his family. "But to all who did receive him, who believed in his name, he gave the right to become children of God, who were born, not of blood nor of the will of the flesh nor of the will of man, but of God" (John 1:12–13). By nature, we are born in sin, wholly separated from God, but in Christ, we are adopted into God's family. Paul says, "But when the fullness of time had come, God sent forth his Son, born of woman, born under the law, to redeem those who were under the law, so that we might receive adoption as sons" (Gal. 4:4–5).

Reading the New Testament is like looking through a family picture album or hearing the family history recited by a grandparent. The church is God's household and our family.

Defining Home

The church is defined by many words and phrases that identify her as being of heavenly origin. The English word *church* originates from the Greek term *kyriakos*, referring to those who belong to the Lord. This word derives from the Greek word *kyrios*, a title given to God as the sovereign Master over a people. The church is, therefore, God's special possession over which he resides as Master.

The Old Testament promise "I will . . . be your God, and you shall be my people" demonstrates that God's people belong to him. Israel was called the flock of God and the choice vine of his vineyard (Jer. 2:21; 23:3). The New Testament transitions that same imagery to Christ and his church. Christ is the shepherd; the church is the flock (Heb. 13:20). Christ is the vine; the church is the branches (John 15:5). Christ is the head; the church is the body (Col. 1:18). Christ is the bridegroom; the church is the bride (Eph. 5:22–27). Christ is not ashamed to call his church his "brothers" (Heb. 2:11), and "God is not ashamed to be called their God" (Heb. 11:16). God has always identified with his people and has jealously claimed them as his own. The church belongs to him and is his home through Christ.

The church is most regularly associated with the Greek word *ekklēsia*, a term meaning "those who are called out" or "an assembly of the people." For instance, the word is used in Matthew 16:18 when Jesus pronounces to Peter, "I tell you, you are Peter, and on this rock I will build my church, and the gates of hell shall not prevail against it." The interpretation of this verse, though debated for centuries, is quite clear. Christ is the Rock upon which the church is founded. She has no power in herself but is called out by the gospel of Christ from among all the peoples of the earth to be eternally established upon "the Son of the living God" (Matt. 16:16–17). The insight of Wilhelmus à Brakel is beneficial here. He brings this rich definition of the church into a crisp sentence: "This one church is made up of all the elect who have been called from the beginning of the world and are yet to be called until the end of the world."[1]

In Ephesians 1, Paul classifies the church with exhilarating phrases that designate just how precious she is to God. Though the words lend themselves to an individual context, Paul is addressing the church as a whole. Therefore, we can use these phrases to arrive at a clearer picture of exactly who the church is:

- "blessed in Christ" (v. 3)
- chosen "before the foundation of the world" (v. 4)
- made "holy and blameless" (v. 4)
- "predestined" by his love (v. 5)
- adopted as "sons through Jesus Christ" (v. 5)
- lavished with the riches of grace (vv. 6–8)
- given an "inheritance" (v. 11)
- are to the "praise of his glory" (v. 12)
- "sealed with the promised Holy Spirit" (v. 13)

From these glorious texts a God-centered definition of the church emerges: The church is uniquely those who have been called out of sinful darkness by God the Father through salvation in Jesus Christ, are now sealed by the Holy Spirit, and now belong to the Lord. The church thus finds her origin, beauty, and perfection in the triune God. And lest she becomes prideful after understanding her position, Paul concludes Ephesians 1 by reminding the church that "he [God] put all things under his [Christ's] feet and gave him as head over all things to the church, which is his body, the fullness of him who fills all in all" (vv. 22–23). As the

---

1 Wilhelmus à Brakel, *The Christian's Reasonable Service*, vol. 2 (Grand Rapids, MI: Reformation Heritage, 2015), 5.

dwelling place and household of God, the church is now under his sole authority.

The Assembly of Mount Zion

Throughout his voluminous works, John Owen, a seventeenth-century Puritan theologian, offers several images and descriptions of the church. In his 1645 *Greater Catechism*, he answers the question "What is the church?" this way: "The whole company of God's elect, called of God, by the Word and Spirit, out of their natural condition, to the dignity of his children, and united unto Christ their head, by faith, in the bond of the Spirit."[2] Consistent with Paul's detailed description of those who are the church in Ephesians 1, Owen is careful to characterize the church as a Trinitarian and heavenly family made up of those whom God elects, calls, and unites to Christ through his lavish grace.

In an exposition of Isaiah 56:7, ". . . my house shall be called a house of prayer for all peoples," Owen expands his catechism response in affirming two ways in which he interprets the church:

> By the church of Christ I understand, *primarily*, the whole multitude of them who antecedently are chosen of his Father, and given unto him; consequently, are redeemed, called, and justified in his blood. . . . And, *secondarily*, also every holy assembly of mount Zion, whereunto the Lord Christ is made beauty and glory, every particular church of his saints, inasmuch as they partake of the nature of the whole, being purchased by his blood.[3]

---

2   John Owen, *The Works of John Owen*, ed. William H. Goold, 24 vols. (1850–1855; repr., vols. 1–16, Edinburgh: Banner of Truth, 1965–1968), 1:485. See also Sinclair Ferguson, *John Owen on the Christian Life* (Edinburgh: Banner of Truth, 1987), 158.

3   Owen, *Works*, 8:286.

THE HOUSEHOLD OF GOD

The church isn't merely a local body of believers gathering on Sundays. The church is the "holy assembly of mount Zion" gathered from every tribe, tongue, and people. And within this assembly, Christ is made beautiful and glorious because they have been purchased through his righteousness and are now members of his family.

In yet another work published in 1681, Owen defines the church this way:

> An especial society or congregation of professed believers, joined together according unto his mind, with their officers, guides, or rulers, whom he hath appointed, which do or may meet together for the celebration of all the ordinances of divine worship, the professing and authoritatively proposing the doctrine of the gospel, with the exercise of the discipline prescribed by himself, unto their own mutual edification, with the glory of Christ, in the preservation and propagation of his kingdom in the world.[4]

Owen is always concerned with identifying those who belong in the church, those within the household of God. Essentially, the church consists of those chosen, called, and faithful. To be a Christian is synonymous with being the church. The two are inseparably and eternally linked. While it's possible to be a member of a church and not be a true follower of Christ, it's impossible to be a genuine believer and not be *in* the church.

By definition, the church is constituted in a particular form. Various characteristics mark her: celebration of worship, preaching of the gospel, the exercise of discipline, mutual edification, and the work of evangelism.[5] The church is best defined by both universal

4 Owen, *Works*, 15:262.
5 Ferguson, *John Owen*, 159.

and local terminology. Theologians sometimes refer to these two categories as "invisible" and "visible." The invisible church is composed of believers worldwide, who have been elected, called, and regenerated. The visible church is those redeemed believers within a local congregation.

God calls and graciously saves individuals to make his home among them within his church. Trying to sever a follower of Christ from the church is like trying to delete the DNA shared by a parent and child. God places us within his larger family, where we obtain a Father in God, a brother in Christ, a Helper in the Spirit, and brothers and sisters with fellow believers. The church is God's household and our home.

God's Home, Forever

It can be quite disheartening when we thoroughly examine the numerous faults, grievous sins, and colossal failures of the church. Some might even warn that God is on the cusp of withdrawing his glory from the church, much like he did from Israel of old (1 Sam. 4:21). Doctrine is on the decline. Interest in God's word waxes cold. Church members are becoming increasingly more interested in temporal than eternal matters. To all present appearances, it would seem that the church has grown lukewarm and lost its first love.

Our one hope is the constant abiding presence of God—forever—which assures the church that God has not forsaken, nor will he ever forsake, his home. He will never love the church any less than he always has. He will never divorce the church. He will never go searching for a more attractive family. He will never move out or move away. The cascade of his love to her will never dissolve, for it runs from eternity past to eternity future.

Consequently, the church confidently proclaims:

And though this world, with devils filled,
should threaten to undo us,
we will not fear, for God has willed
his truth to triumph through us.
The prince of darkness grim,
we tremble not for him;
his rage we can endure,
for lo! his doom is sure;
one little word shall fell him.

That Word above all earthly powers
no thanks to them abideth;
the Spirit and the gifts are ours
through him who with us sideth.
Let goods and kindred go,
this mortal life also;
the body they may kill:
God's truth abideth still;
his kingdom is forever![6]

God doesn't begrudgingly give himself to the church. He doesn't bemoan the home he has made among us. He doesn't regret pursuing us with his everlasting love. God delights to make the church his household and makes her beautiful by his presence among her. She can unwaveringly trust that

the dwelling place of God is with man. He will dwell with them, and they will be his people, and God himself will be with them

---

6 Martin Luther, "A Mighty Fortress Is Our God," 1529, trans. Frederick H. Hedge, 1852; accessed July 29, 2021, https://hymnary.org.

as their God. He will wipe away every tear from their eyes, and death shall be no more, neither shall there be mourning, nor crying, nor pain anymore, for the former things have passed away. (Rev. 21:3–4)

3

Our Father and Friend

O LORD, you are our Father;
we are the clay, and you are the potter;
we are all the work of your hand.

ISAIAH 64:8

THE CHURCH BELONGS TO GOD. She is his treasure and consists of his children and friends. The last chapter defined the church as the dwelling place of God. He promised, "I will walk among you and will be your God, and you shall be my people" (Lev. 26:12).

To define the church as a mere earthly institution or some entrepreneur's vision would be to miss completely who the church is in God's eternal mind and heart. The church's beauty comes into indefectible focus only when we peer through the lens of God's relationship to her. Anything less is choosing to play in mud puddles while refusing the vastness of the ocean.

The church was never God's plan B. Even when Adam and Eve fell in the garden in Genesis 3 and introduced sin into the perfection of God's creation, the church was still the trajectory of God's redemptive plan (Eph. 1:4). By making us the object of his divine love through Christ, God differentiates himself as our Father and friend.

Our Father

In Matthew 6, the disciples request that Jesus teach them how to pray. Jesus offers them something entirely unexpected to their old covenant way of thinking. He constructs a short prayer that serves as a pattern for all our conversations with God. While the prayer contains all the elements one might expect, Jesus addresses God using a personal name somewhat foreign to the Old Testament theological mind.

Under the old covenant, the children of God approached him in fear and trembling through the ritualism of priesthood and sacrifice. To enter his holy presence, the Israelites were required to meet with God through the tabernacle and temple. If they dared approach God in any other way, the consequences could have been severe. Nadab and Abihu, Aaron's two sons, thought they would be creative and offered "strange fire," which God had not allowed. Immediately, "fire came out from before the LORD and consumed them, and they died before the LORD" (Lev. 10:1–2 with marginal trans.).

The Jewish people often understood the fatherhood of God in a national sense but seldom in a personal relationship. God is the Creator of all things, made man in his divine image, and sovereignly directs the course of history, but can we personally know him? Though great fear and trepidation often filled the Old Testament worshiper, there are glimpses of God's familial nearness to his people, as we find expressed through the prophet Jeremiah:

> Is Ephraim my dear son?
> Is he my darling child?
> For as often as I speak against him,

I do remember him still.
Therefore my heart yearns for him;
I will surely have mercy on him,
    declares the LORD. (31:20)

Here we are offered a small window into the fatherly love of
Israel's God.

Though God was as much of a Father to believers in the Old Testament as he is in the New, Jesus brings God eternally close to the heart
of the believer and invites us to bypass the priests, animal sacrifices,
veils, and temples by offering us a vividly affectionate relationship
with the sovereign of the universe: "Our Father in heaven" (Matt. 6:9).

An eternity would not be long enough to mine all the illustrious
riches from the title "Our Father." With that seemingly simple name,
beautifully familiar and astonishingly personal, Jesus brings God from a
distant celestial realm into the mundane everyday life of ordinary people.

The most common name for God throughout Scripture is Yahweh. Appearing more than sixty-eight hundred times throughout
the Old Testament, it speaks of God's unchangeable, eternal nature
and separates him from all other gods as the everlasting "I AM." In
Exodus 3, when Moses requests that God tell him his name, God
responds by saying, "I AM WHO I AM" and "I AM" (vv. 13–15), and
then he identifies "LORD" (Yahweh) as his "name forever" (v. 15).

Peculiarly, when Jesus teaches his people to pray, he addresses God
not as Yahweh, or even Elohim (God), Tsur (Rock of Israel), or the
common Adonai (my Lord), but as Father (*ab*). Both in Matthew 6 and
throughout the other Gospel record, Jesus's name for God is strikingly
unassuming and down-to-earth: "Father." Jesus offers his church the same
close personal name to use for God as he uses himself. Because God is
Jesus's Father, we also have the tremendous benefit of calling him Father.

The word Jesus uses for "Father" is probably the Aramaic word *abba*. It's the most affectionate and warm of the ancient names for a father. Jesus uses it to identify the relationship God has with his children. A term used by children both young and old, it denotes love and affection. Perhaps you remember the first time your own child constructed the syllables to utter the precious word *Daddy* or *Mommy*. The utterance of this unadorned and straightforward name causes a parent's heart to swell with joy.

God is the Father to his children in a way he is not to anyone else. When your child screams "Daddy!" or "Mommy!" in a crowd of people, you immediately spin on your heels to the attention of that little voice. Your child doesn't say your proper name, but you instinctively recognize that cry versus everyone else's. How? Because your children are yours, and you are theirs. Only God's children who know him in Christ are allowed the privilege of calling him Father. Jesus gives this benefit to his church alone.

God isn't only *a* Father or *the* Father, but he is *our* Father. He uniquely loves his church. John Owen described the Father's love as "the fountain from whence all other sweetnesses flow."[1] Owen differentiates the Father's devotion to his people as uniquely exalted above all earthly love:

> *Eternal.* It was fixed on us before the foundation of the world. Before we were, or had done the least good, then were his thoughts upon us. . . .
>
> *Free.* He loves us because he will; there was, there is, nothing in us for which we should be beloved. . . .

---

1   John Owen, *The Works of John Owen*, ed. William H. Goold, 24 vols. (1850–1855; repr., vols. 1–16, Edinburgh: Banner of Truth, 1965–1968), 2:22.

Unchangeable. Though we change every day, yet his love changeth not. . . .

Distinguishing. He hath not thus loved all the world. . . . Why should he fix his love on us, and pass by millions from whom we differ not by nature?[2]

The love of the Father always precedes our love toward him. "We love [God] because he first loved us" (1 John 4:19). Our Father's love isn't reluctant or dependent upon how many we have sitting in our church pews, how many turn up for evangelism training, or how quickly our church grows. Sometimes the church thinks the Father's love waxes and wanes according to the benefits, gifts, and blessings he gives or withholds. Owen wrote:

> It is the love of him who is in himself all-sufficient, infinitely satisfied with himself and his own glorious excellencies and perfections; who has no need to go forth with his love unto others, nor to seek an object of it without [outside] himself. . . . He had his Son, also his eternal Wisdom, to rejoice and delight himself in from all eternity.[3]

The Father's love proceeds from his abundant satisfaction and joy in his Son, not out of loneliness or need for others to fulfill him. If we could put it in these terms: The church isn't lovely because she warrants love from God. The church is lovely because the Father loves her through Christ, who is her mediator (1 Tim. 2:5).

What does it mean for the church to call God "our Father"?

First, it's the end of self-exaltation. To confess that God is our Father is to acknowledge that we are helpless creatures and cannot rescue

2 Owen, *Works*, 2:33–34.
3 Owen, *Works*, 2:32.

ourselves, for we need a Father who watches over us to save, protect, guide, and help. The church is sometimes a stage upon which men and women boast about good works or parade supposed self-righteousness. To call God "our Father" is to confess that any good in ministry proceeding from our hands flows directly from him, for he is "able to do far more abundantly than all that we ask or think, according to the power at work with us" (Eph. 3:20). Therefore, any glory for what takes place within the church belongs alone to God (Ps. 115:1).

Second, calling God "our Father" means that specific fears should cease. To enter into a loving relationship with a loving Father through a loving Son eliminates any fear we could ever have of the wrath of God against our sin. In our stead, Jesus drank the full cup of God's wrath against our sin to give us a Father. Furthermore, to utter these precious words eliminates any fear we may have of man (Matt. 10:28). This is utterly freeing for the church and allows her to be a bold worshiping witness at the very gates of hell itself. After all, she recognizes that man can do nothing to her because she has God as a Father.

Third, to call God "our Father" brings an end to our hopelessness. There's no greater hope that children can have in a life wrecked by sin, shame, and despair than to be in the arms of a devoted, loving heavenly Father. This truth reminds his church that heaven and earth will pass away before any of his specific plans for her will ever be thwarted. While we don't know those plans in detail, we can minister in buoyant hope that he has planned to carry his church all the way home. Additionally, our hope resides in the promise that he will hear our prayers (1 John 5:14). There is no greater power that the church possesses than to converse with our heavenly Father. Knowing he hears us and answers us according to his eternal will causes all hopelessness to vanish like the fog before the blazing sun. For God has granted to his children "the riches of the glory of this mystery, which is Christ in you, the hope of glory" (Col. 1:27).

It's also an end of loneliness. As our Father, God grants the church an intimacy and relationship with him that is all her own. That relationship began before the foundation of the world when God chose to set his everlasting love upon us in Christ. It's all too easy for a local congregation to feel isolated and alone. Particularly in seasons of political upheaval or pandemic restrictions, the church can be a lonely place to serve. But our identity as his children grants us immediate access to a Father who has promised never to leave us or forsake us (Heb. 13:5).

Is there anyone who knows all our failures and still loves us? Is there anyone who can give meaning to our hopeless lives? Is there anyone who can run to our rescue when we've scraped our knees and can't get up? Is there anyone who can encourage us when we want to throw in the ministry towel? Is there anyone who can wipe away rolling tears? Our Father can.

Jesus said in Luke 12:32, "Fear not, little flock, for it is your Father's good pleasure to give you the kingdom." If the Father has promised to give us his kingdom, will he not guide, direct, nurture, help, comfort, and lead our local congregations? Richard Sibbes wrote:

> When all is taken from us in losses and crosses . . . our fathers may die, and our mothers may die, and our nearest, and dearest friends . . . may die; but we have a Father of mercy, that hath eternal mercy in him, his mercies are tender mercies, and everlasting mercies, as himself is. . . . When all are taken away, God takes not himself away, he is the Father of mercy still.[4]

---

4 Richard Sibbes, *Works of Richard Sibbes*, ed. Alexander B. Grosart, 7 vols. (1862–1864; repr., Edinburgh: Banner of Truth , 1978–1983), 3:68.

Our Friend

As children, we all liked to pronounce over someone that he or she was our "best friend." Though that place of honor usually changed weekly, just the simple title was a badge of pride. It meant that a particular person was your confidant, someone to whom you could reveal your darkest secret, and also one who rejoiced at your greatest triumph. This person was more than a mere acquaintance or even a regular friend; here was your *best* friend.

The church consists of God's friends.

After God had established his covenant with Abraham, the patriarch was called "the *friend* of God" (2 Chron. 20:7; cf. Gen. 17:7). God himself declared in Isaiah 41:8,

> But you, Israel, my servant,
>> Jacob, whom I have chosen,
>>> the offspring of Abraham, *my friend*. . . .

When we come to the New Testament, James affirms that Abraham "was called a *friend* of God" (James 2:23). Abraham wasn't searching or seeking for God but was a beneficiary of God's sovereign friendship. The intimacy of Abraham's friendship with God flourished when Abraham left his tent to walk with the angels toward the city of Sodom, which they were about to destroy. The Lord said, "Shall I hide from Abraham what I am about to do?" (Gen. 18:17). Because God was Abraham's friend, he disclosed secrets that he would tell no one else. This friendly confidence is no different with the rest of God's people. God not only has revealed to us his word in the Bible but also has provided the inward residence and illumination of his Holy Spirit that we may rightly understand what he has revealed. As a result, it is said of the church, "You have been anointed by the Holy One, and you all have knowledge" (1 John 2:20).[5]

Genuine friendship is more than action; it's devotion. When this devotion is the lens through which the church views God's company with us, that reality is so inexhaustible that it defies comprehension. God's benevolent offering of his beloved Son is most brightly on display in the Son's willingness to offer his life a ransom for his Father's friends: "Greater love has no one than this, that someone lay down his life for his friends" (John 15:13). And since the Father freely gave us his beloved Son, "how will he not also with him graciously give us all things?" (Rom. 8:32).

Unlike a school playground friend, God holds his friends beautifully close to his heart from everlasting to everlasting. He doesn't abandon his church for a better or more faithful or more loyal friend. He's never lamented choosing the church as his friend. When God established his friendship with the church, it had absolutely nothing to do with our faithfulness to him and everything to do with his faithfulness to us. He comforts his friends by reminding them,

> The mountains may depart
> and the hills be removed,
> but my steadfast love shall not depart from you,
> and my covenant of peace shall not be removed. (Isa. 54:10)

Through the millennia of the church's existence, her history often paints a disturbing picture of unfaithfulness, coldness, error, lethargy, and the like. But her friendship with God gives the church great comfort that though she may wander off the path at certain junctures,

---

5   R. B. Kuiper, *The Glorious Body of Christ* (London: Banner of Truth, 1966), 335.

he always remains her faithful friend. The writer of Hebrews reminds us of God's consoling words to the weeping prophet "I will be their God, and they shall be my people" (Jer. 31:31–33; Heb. 8:8–10). There has never been a time in her patchy history, nor will there be a time in her future, when God will deny his friend, forsake his friend, or cast his friend aside. When earthly friends disappoint us in their commitment and devotion, we know we can sing of God:

> I've found a Friend, oh, such a Friend!
> He loved me ere I knew Him,
> And drew me with the cords of love,
> And thus He bound me to Him.
> And round my heart still closely twine
> Those ties which naught can sever,
> For I am His, and He is mine
> Forever and ever.[6]

God is both a Father and a friend to the church. These cherished relationships remind the church that God isn't remote and distant but is near and close. As the hymn above proclaims, he "drew me with the cords of love, / and thus He bound me to Him." We are eternally bound to our Father and friend. He is uniquely ours, and we are uniquely his. This is why God sent his Son. Jesus brings God near to us; Jesus brings God down to us; Jesus brings God into us. We could also reverse the order: Jesus brings us near to God; Jesus brings us up to God; Jesus brings us to God. No greater privilege has been given to the church than being able to call God, through Christ, "our Father" and "our Friend."

---

6   James G. Small, "I've Found a Friend; O Such a Friend!," 1866.

4

Our Savior and Head

Christ is the head of the church,
his body, and is himself its Savior.

EPHESIANS 5:23

TO GRASP CHRIST'S LOVE for his church is to plumb depths that
have no bottom, find a treasure with no bounds, and climb heights
that have no peak. As believers, we never move past the love of Christ.
We never tire of the love of Christ. A true believer is one who never
gets over the profound words of the childhood song "Jesus loves me!
This I know, for the Bible tells me so."

All of our redemption and salvation flows freely from that
never-ending fountain of divine love. And such boundless love
can only rightly be understood by visiting a bloody cross and an
empty tomb.

With an interleafed blank Bible before him to write down his
endless meditations, Jonathan Edwards savored the love of Christ:
"Everything that was contrived and done for the redemption and
salvation of believers, and every benefit they have by it, is wholly

and perfectly from the free, eternal, distinguishing love and infinite grace of Christ towards them."[1]

Everything we have as the church. Everything we are as the church. Everything we could ever hope to be as the church. Everything— wrapped up in the "free, eternal, distinguishing love and infinite grace of Christ."

This infinite love is comprehensive and causes the bridegroom to rescue his bride from the depths of her sin and depravity by taking his lover's place at the bar of holy judgment. Greater than spinning the worlds into existence is this selfless act of sacrifice that makes Jesus both a Savior and head of his church.

Our Savior

Many titles used of Christ are also used interchangeably of God the Father. One of the Father's exalted titles in the Old Testament is "God our Savior," or more literally "the God of our salvation." God is a rescuer and deliverer of his people. In Isaiah 49:26, he proclaims,

> All flesh shall know
>> that I am the LORD your Savior,
>> and your Redeemer, the Mighty One of Jacob.

The hymnody of the Psalms repeatedly ascribes the same title to God:

- "You are the God of my salvation" (Ps. 25:5).
- "Make haste to help me, / O Lord, my salvation!" (Ps. 38:22).
- "By awesome deeds you answer . . . / O God of our salvation" (Ps. 65:5).

---

1 Jonathan Edwards, *The "Blank Bible,"* ed. Stephen J. Stein, vol. 24 of *The Works of Jonathan Edwards* (New Haven, CT: Yale University Press, 2006), 617.

- "Help us, O God of our salvation" (Ps. 79:9).
- "Restore us again, O God of our salvation" (Ps. 85:4).

When we come to the opening chapters of the New Testament, just so we don't miss his divinity, God repeatedly reminds us that his incarnate Son is a Savior. At the beginning of Mary's Magnificat, she worshipfully cries, "My spirit rejoices in God my Savior" (Luke 1:47). The angel who appears to Joseph triumphantly announces that Jesus will be the one to "save his people from their sins" (Matt. 1:21). The angels announce to the shepherds in the fields, "Unto you is born this day in the city of David a Savior, who is Christ the Lord" (Luke 2:11).

The Greek word translated "Savior" means "one who preserves or rescues from natural dangers and afflictions." It carries the idea of deliverance from harm in order to preserve. A Savior is both a rescuer and protector. In his prophecy of the Messiah, Zechariah affirms that this anointed one will deliver us from the "hand of our enemies" (Luke 1:74).

Who are our enemies, and why do we need rescuing?

We need rescuing from our sin, God's wrath upon our sin, and death, which is a consequence of our sin. The prophet said,

Your iniquities have made a separation
    between you and your God,
and your sins have hidden his face from you. (Isa. 59:2)

God is so holy that he cannot look upon sin, approve of sin, or accept sinful creatures into his presence (Hab. 1:13).

Paul clearly defines the consequences of sin as death (Rom. 6:23). "For all have sinned and fall short of the glory of God" (Rom. 3:23). Paul laments: "Wretched man that I am! Who will deliver me from this body of death?" (Rom. 7:24). He answers his question in 1 Thessalonians 1:10, "Jesus who delivers us from the wrath to come."

In Luke 15:1–7, Jesus tells the parable of a shepherd who leaves his flock to search for the one lost sheep. Jesus is the shepherd who rescues his bride from the sinful shackles of death. Jesus is the one who delivers his bride from God's holy wrath upon sin. He is our Savior, and the stage upon which that glorious rescuing work is accomplished is his cross and tomb. The bride identifies with the cross and the tomb because they are *her* cross and tomb.

Jesus doesn't just excuse our sin and tell us to never mind its consequences. Christ and his bride are so intimately identified that they become united with one another in death and resurrection. Sinners come to the cross of Christ and receive, by faith, the wages of their sin—death. We don't die physically, but we die a required death through Christ, for he becomes our substitute and stands in our stead, taking upon himself the unmitigated wrath of his Father. What God requires of us, because of our sin, is paid in full by our beloved, the Lord Jesus Christ.

The cross, with all of its blood flowing, lacerated flesh, and the stench of death, becomes the epicenter of cleansing for sinners, where Christ looks lovingly upon his darling bride and declares,

My love . . .
    you are beautiful. (Song 1:15)

The tomb, with all its miraculous power, folded grave clothes, and heavenly promises, becomes the same power by which dead sinners emerge from their sin, having been raised to new life through Christ.

When Jesus died on the cross, we died on the cross.

When Jesus rose from the dead, we rose from the dead.

This beautiful union is so fixed and permanent that we are now taken into the eternal love that exists between the Father and the Son through the Spirit. The same love that flows unceasingly between the Father and the Son now directly flows to the bride.

In a masterful sermon on the work of the Holy Spirit, Edwards defines this union as existing in two parts: Christ is united to us in nature, and Christ is united to us in love.[2] First, he says: "Christ was united to us in nature. By his incarnation, he took our nature upon him, and by that wonderful act of his, united himself to us. He manifested his gracious and wonderful design of becoming the head of the human nature, the head of all the elect of mankind."[3] Christ became like us. The writer of Hebrews says, "He had to be made like his brothers in every respect, so that he might become a merciful and faithful high priest in the service of God, to make propitiation for the sins of the people" (Heb. 2:17). If Christ were not united to us in nature, he could not be our Savior.

Also, Christ is united to us in love. Edwards writes, "Christ loves the elect with so great and strong a love, they are so near to him, that God looks upon them as it were as parts of him."[4] Because of our union with Christ, God's love of him now includes love of his bride. We become sole recipients of the love that has forever flowed between the Father, Son, and Spirit.

Jesus is a worthy Savior not only because of his union with the nature and love of his Father but also because of union with the nature and

---

2   Jonathan Edwards, *Sermons and Discourses, 1723–1729*, ed. Kenneth P. Minkema, vol. 14 of *The Works of Jonathan Edwards* (New Haven, CT: Yale University Press, 1997), 403. See also Oliver D. Crisp and Kyle C. Strobel, *Jonathan Edwards: An Introduction to His Thought* (Grand Rapids, MI: Eerdmans, 2018).

3   Edwards, *Sermons and Discourses, 1723–1729*, 403.

4   Edwards, *Sermons and Discourses, 1723–1729*, 403.

love of his bride. He unites to her as she places her faith in him and thus he becomes the ground of her rescue and redemption. The bridegroom takes death upon himself and offers his meritorious work freely to his bride, that she may be welcomed into his glorious dwelling, the church.

Our Head

The relationship between Christ and his bride is so multifaceted that merely one title will not satisfy all its beauty. Numerous rich metaphors throughout Scripture depict this divine exchange:

- Christ is both her founder and her foundation.
- Christ is both her Judge and her Savior.
- Christ is both her lover and her beloved.
- Christ is both her preserver and her hope.
- Christ is both her righteousness and her holiness.

However, perhaps no metaphorical phrase comes close to the gravity of Christ being the *head* of the church. Uniting himself to us in our nature not only makes Jesus a fit Savior for his bride but also makes him a fit head. Edwards helps us here as well.

> Christ was united to us in nature. . . . He thereby is near of kin to us, he is become our elder brother. Yea, more than a brother: by that act of taking the human nature upon himself, he sufficiently in the sight of God and in the sight of angels assumed the elect part of mankind into an union with himself, and was justly looked upon as their head.

Now, as both her bridegroom and her representative elder brother in salvation, Christ is the head of all believers. And since all believers are now part of the body of Christ, he is the head of his church.

The phrase "head of the church" is not employed to identify Christ as the head of a company or the head of an organization. In Ephesians 5:23, Paul distinguishes Christ as "the head of the church, *his body*." The church isn't the result of human ingenuity. The living Christ is the head of a living organism. This emblematic language is used throughout Paul's epistles:

I want you to understand that the *head* of every man is Christ. (1 Cor. 11:3)

And he put all things under his feet and gave him as *head* over all things to the church, which is his body. (Eph. 1:22–23)

Speaking the truth in love, we are to grow up in every way into him who is the *head*, into Christ. (Eph. 4:15)

Christ is the *head* of the church, his body, and is himself its Savior. (Eph. 5:23)

He is the *head* of the body, the church. (Col. 1:18)

And not holding fast to the *Head*, from whom the whole body, nourished and knit together through its joints and ligaments, grows with a growth that is from God. (Col. 2:19)

R. B. Kuiper writes: "The gist of these passages is that the relationship between Christ as the Head and the church as his body is organic. . . . The organic union of Christ and his church is a profound mystery. Therefore, he who seeks to describe it must exercise the greatest care to speak soberly."[5] Identifying Christ as the church's head denotes that he has sovereign lordship and supreme authority

---

5   R. B. Kuiper, *The Glorious Body of Christ* (London: Banner of Truth, 1966), 93.

over her. As Jesus told his disciples when he commissioned them to evangelize the nations, "All authority in heaven and on earth has been given to me" (Matt. 28:18).

This singular authority residing in Christ is not only a New Testament concept. The prophecies of the Old Testament also speak of the Messiah as possessing absolute authority. In Daniel 7:13–14, the exiled prophet says of Christ:

I saw in the night visions,

and behold, with the clouds of heaven
    there came one like a son of man,
and he came to the Ancient of Days
    and was presented before him.
And to him was given dominion
    and glory and a kingdom,
that all peoples, nations, and languages
    should serve him;
his dominion is an everlasting dominion,
    which shall not pass away,
and his kingdom one
    that shall not be destroyed.

The supremacy of Jesus was firmly established before creation, was exhibited during his incarnation, reigns now over his church, and will be eternally established upon his return.

The church receives all of its life from Christ and has no life apart from him—they are one. As one cannot live without unremitting oxygen intake, the church cannot exist for one moment without Christ as her life. Christ is the church's ventilator—consistently filling her lungs with life-giving spiritual breath animating her, gifting her, and empowering her. This means that we who serve in the church serve her only as Christ empowers and enables us to do so. It means that Christ imparted to the church, and will continue to impart to her, his very life.

In a sermon delivered on November 1, 1868, Charles Spurgeon asks, "What is the church?" His answer materializes out of the glorious reality of Christ as her head:

> What is the church? The word signifies an assembly. The church of Jesus Christ is an assembly of faithful men, the whole company of God's chosen, and called out ones, the entire community of true followers of the Lord Jesus Christ. Wherever true believers are, there is a part of the church; wherever such men are not, whatever organisation may be in existence, there is no church of Jesus Christ. The church is no corporation of priests, or confederacy of unconverted men, it is the assembly of those whose names are written in heaven. Any assembly of faithful men is *a* church. The aggregate of all these assemblies of faithful men make up *the* one church which Jesus Christ has redeemed with his most precious blood, and of which he is the sole and only Head. Part of that church is in heaven, triumphant, part on earth, militant, but these differences of place make no division concerning real unity; there is only one church above and below. Time creates no separation, the church is always one—one church of the apostles, one church of the reformers, one church of the first century, one church of the latter days, and of this one and only church Jesus Christ is the one and only Head.[6]

6　Charles H. Spurgeon, "The Head of the Church" (sermon, November 1, 1868), in *The Metropolitan Tabernacle Pulpit: Containing Sermons Preached and Revised*, vol. 14 (Pasadena, TX: Pilgrim, 1982), 613–24.

Within Spurgeon's definition of the church is the underlying reality of Christ as her life and head, for without him she can do nothing (John 15:5).

Paul illustrates Christ as the church's head by using the unfathomable relationship between a husband and a wife. In Ephesians 5:23, the wife's primary motive for submitting to her husband's authority is that he is her functioning head in the family, just as Christ is the church's functioning head. The implication is that the wife who doesn't fulfill her spiritual responsibility to submit to her husband's leadership causes dysfunction in the family. On the other hand, a wife who lovingly responds to her head's direction brings honor to her family, husband, and, most importantly, her Lord. She becomes a testimony to the world of how the church is to appropriately respond to Christ in submission, honor, and service. This is a relationship not of oppression but of liberating freedom in being who God has called us to be. Paul points to the family as the pattern for the church.

How does Christ head his church?

He does it through the instrumentality of godly leaders (1 Thess. 5:12–13; Heb. 13:7, 17). Pastors, elders, and deacons are representatives of Christ's authority over the church. Paul summarizes the purpose of these shepherds this way: "to equip the saints for the work of ministry, for building up of the body of Christ" (Eph. 4:11–12). Kuiper clarifies that "while [Christ] does *delegate* authority to them, he never *transfers* to them the authority which is his."[7] Therefore, any supposed authority the leaders of the church possess is a delegated authority from Christ. It is always Christ, and Christ alone, who governs the church. The sole responsibility of those given charge in

7   Kuiper, *The Glorious Body of Christ*, 94.

leading, teaching, preaching, and serving her is to declare and apply the instructions of Christ as revealed in his written word.

Not only does Christ exercise his headship through godly leaders, but he also governs his church through his word and Spirit. The primary function of a pastor-shepherd is to feed the flock of God by serving them the nourishing food of God's word (2 Tim. 3:16–17; 1 Pet. 2:2–3). Through preaching and teaching, the Holy Spirit draws people to himself and enlarges and nurtures God's family.

The headship of Christ not only extends to the church but also encompasses "all things" (Eph. 1:22). Only Christ can protect the church against our adversary, the devil, the temptations of our fallen flesh, and the lies of the world. Only Christ can fulfill his promise that the gates of hell will never prevail against her. Only Christ can gather his sheep and grow his church. Only Christ can bring us all the way to his marriage supper.

In a well-known story, the wife of one of the generals of King Cyrus of Persia is accused of treachery and condemned to die. As soon as her husband realizes what has taken place, he rushes to the palace and bursts into the throne room. Throwing himself on the floor before the king, he cries out: "O king, take my life instead of hers. Let me die in her place." Cyrus, by all historical accounts a noble and extremely sensitive man, is touched by this offer and replies, "Love like that must not be spoiled by death." And so he gives the husband and wife back to each other, letting the wife go free. As the two walk away happily, the husband says to his wife, "Did you notice how kindly the king looked upon us when he gave you the pardon?" The wife replies: "I had no eyes for the king. I saw only the man who was willing to die in my place."[8]

---

8 William J. McRae, *Preparing for Your Marriage* (Grand Rapids, MI: Zondervan, 1980), 98.

The church is intimately united to Christ as her Savior and head. This glorious truth will be the theme of the new song the bride will trumpet forth throughout the heavens:

> Worthy are you to take the scroll
>> and to open its seals,
> for you were slain, and by your blood you ransomed people
>> for God
>> from every tribe and language and people and nation.
>> (Rev. 5:9)

5

Our Helper and Beautifier

I will ask the Father, and he will give you another Helper.

JOHN 14:16

ANY DISCUSSION ON THE CHURCH would be severely lacking without a close look at the presence and ministry of the Holy Spirit. Without him, the church would never have been founded. Godly leaders would never have been called, believers added, gifts distributed, service rendered, or growth realized.

The Holy Spirit is mentioned some fifty-six times in the book of Acts as filling, helping, guiding, calling, aiding, growing, sanctifying, maturing, organizing, assisting, regenerating, teaching, testifying to, interceding for, reminding, grieving over, and loving believers, who make up the church. Without the ministry of the Holy Spirit, there is no church. But with the ministry of the Holy Spirit, the church shines forth beautifully as he makes her his glorious dwelling.

Our Helper

To comfort the hearts of his despondent disciples, who have just learned that Jesus will soon be leaving them, he promises them a

"Helper" (John 14:16). Jesus unveils the identity and ministry of this divine Helper in subsequent verses:

> The Helper, the Holy Spirit, whom the Father will send in my name, he will teach you all things and bring to your remembrance all that I have said to you. (John 14:26)

> When the Helper comes, whom I will send to you from the Father, the Spirit of truth, who proceeds from the Father, he will bear witness about me. (John 15:26)

> Nevertheless, I tell you the truth: it is to your advantage that I go away, for if I do not go away, the Helper will not come to you. But if I go, I will send him to you. (John 16:7)

The Greek word used here in reference to the Holy Spirit is *paraklētos*, which means "one called to another's side, specifically to help and aid." It can also denote an intercessor, an assistant, or someone who pleads another's cause before a judge. The word itself reveals the all-encompassing role of the Spirit within the body of Christ. He is our Helper, Intercessor, Assistant, Advocate, Comforter, Counselor, and Sustainer.

What love Jesus has for the church! He doesn't leave her to fend for herself with her own devices, inventions, creativity, or wit. Surprisingly, he says, "It is to your advantage that I go away" (John 16:7). If we listen closely, we can almost hear the disciples bemoan Jesus's words. "What could possibly be good about you leaving us, Jesus?" Peter is so steadfast in his resolve that Jesus will not be leaving that he takes Jesus aside from the others and rebukes him (Matt. 16:21–23).

Yes, the disciples have a daunting and seemingly insurmountable task of walking in Jesus's footsteps and continuing his ministry on earth. The proclamation of the gospel to the nations, the organization of the church, discipling believers, caring for orphans and widows, and all the rest—"You can't leave us, Jesus! How are we to accomplish all of this?" In his love and comforting care of his disciples, he essentially says, "My Father will give you a Helper."

The Holy Spirit is sufficiently enough to equip and empower you to discharge every aspect of the turning-the-world-upside-down ministry to which Jesus has called his church.

The exaltation of Christ to the right hand of the Father at his ascending enthronement and subsequent sending of the Holy Spirit can clearly be seen as advantageous after a quick survey of a few of the numerous ministries he performs within the church:

- He counsels (Isa. 11:2).
- He imparts wisdom (Isa. 11:2).
- He adopts (Rom. 8:15).
- He calls to ministry (Acts 13:2–4).
- He empowers (Acts 1:8).
- He illuminates (1 Cor. 2:10–13).
- He produces fruit (Gal. 5:22–23).
- He seals (2 Cor. 1:22).
- He strengthens (John 14:26).
- He helps (John 14:16)
- He intercedes (Rom. 8:26).
- He provides truth (John 14:17, 26).
- He teaches (Luke 12:12).
- He testifies (John 15:26).
- He guides (Acts 16:16–17).
- He grieves (Eph. 4:30).

- He convicts (2 Thess. 2:6–7).
- He loves (Rom. 5:5; 15:30).[1]

Our Beautifier

One characteristic we don't often consider, and perhaps have never considered, as a ministry of the Holy Spirit is that of a beautifier. Each of the above ministries is for the purpose of beautifying the church in order to "present the church to himself in splendor, without spot or wrinkle or any such thing, that she might be holy and without blemish" (Eph. 5:27). Like a bride waking up on her wedding day and spending hours perfecting her beauty, every aspect of the Spirit's ministry to, in, and through the church is to make her holier and consequently more beautiful.

Here we benefit again from the wisdom and insight of Jonathan Edwards, who believed sanctification—the inward transformation of our affections to make us more like Jesus—is beautification. That is, being made holy is being made beautiful. In his sermon "God's Excellencies," Edwards preached:

> Holiness is the very beauty and loveliness of Jehovah himself. 'Tis the excellency of his excellencies, the beauty of his beauties, the perfection of his infinite perfections, and the glory of his attributes. What an honor, then, must it be to a creature who is infinitely below God, and less than he, to be beautified and adorned with this beauty, with that beauty which is the highest beauty of God himself, even holiness.[2]

This is the incomparable work of the Holy Spirit in the lives and hearts of every redeemed believer, to make us beautiful by making

---

1   For further investigation into the personhood of the Holy Spirit, see *Biblical Doctrine*, ed. John MacArthur and Richard Mayhue (Wheaton, IL: Crossway, 2017), 334–35.
2   Jonathan Edwards, *Sermons and Discourses, 1720–1723*, ed. Wilson H. Kimnach, vol. 10 of *The Works of Jonathan Edwards* (New Haven, CT: Yale University Press, 1992), 430.

us like Christ. Edwards says we should be amazed that God would make any of his creatures holy, even the unfallen angels, but how much more glorious is it for God to "sanctify sinners—loathsome and abominable creatures—and make them like to himself."[3]

This beautification process begins as we are brought into an intimate relationship with the one who is supremely beautiful and lovely. In John 16:14, Jesus emphasizes that the ministry of the Spirit is not to draw attention to himself but to glorify Christ, "for he will take what is mine and declare it to you." In all his conforming and transforming work in the life of individual believers and the life of the church, the Holy Spirit perpetually points to Jesus.

Glancing at Jesus doesn't make sinners beautiful. Being a mere spectator of a local church doesn't make sinners beautiful. Living on the edge of gospel-centered ministry doesn't make sinners beautiful. The beauty for which we are saved is accomplished only through an intense, heartfelt stare at Jesus. We all know what it's like to receive a glaring stare from a parent when we've disobeyed. Words aren't necessary for a reprimand; the stare alone communicates the required level of conformity. Edwards says we need such a sight of the divine beauty of Christ that our hearts and wills bow before his loveliness. Naturally, as long as our redeemed souls are encased in sinful flesh, we oppose the Spirit's work of beautifying holiness. But "one glimpse of the moral and spiritual glory of God, and supreme amiableness of Jesus Christ, shining into the heart, overcomes and abolishes this opposition, and inclines the soul to Christ."[4] When the Spirit causes the beauty of Christ to dawn in our hearts, all opposition to

---

3 Edwards, *Sermons and Discourses, 1720–1723*, 430.
4 Jonathan Edwards, *Sermons and Discourses, 1743–1758*, ed. Wilson H. Kimnach, vol. 25 of *The Works of Jonathan Edwards* (New Haven, CT: Yale University Press, 2006), 635.

holiness flees, our eyes firmly rivet to his flawless loveliness, and we are made beautiful.

A chief work of the Spirit is to bring beauty out of chaos. In creation, the Spirit brought harmony out of formlessness and void (Gen. 1:2). In redemption, the Spirit brings life out of death and sin (John 3:5–6, 8). In sanctification, the Spirit brings beauty out of fallen flesh and wayward hearts (Rom. 8:9–11). The church becomes an instrument of Christ's beaming radiance in the world through the individual expressions of the work of grace by the Spirit in the lives of believers.

A Beautifying Work

There's perhaps no better or more familiar expression of the Holy Spirit's beautifying work within the church than Galatians 5:22–23, "The fruit of the Spirit is love, joy, peace, patience, kindness, goodness, faithfulness, gentleness, self-control." At our salvation, the Spirit could instantaneously make us holy in action, word, and deed. However, he chooses instead to produce fruit in our lives to authenticate our union with Christ. Bearing fruit is a sign that we are *in* Christ, and he is *in* us. Often the emphasis is wrongly placed on the size of our congregations, the number of baptisms performed in a year, the heft of our offerings, the breadth of our church programs, and the like as evidence of the Spirit's presence. However, Paul makes clear that without the Spirit-produced fruit listed above, all else is vain.

In John 15, Jesus contrasts two branches, one that bears fruit and one that does not. The one that bears fruit is carefully and tenderly pruned, making it viable to bear more abundant fruit. The branch that does not bear fruit is worse than useless and pruned off because it produces no evidence of receiving life-giving nourishment from the root.

The same theme is picked up in Galatians when Paul speaks of the fruit that blooms and ripens to demonstrate the Spirit's habitation within the life of a believer. Paul spends considerable time, in this theologically rich epistle, on the Spirit's work in redemption and sanctification. From the beginning of the Christian life, all the way to glory, the Spirit is working. Paul instructs believers, and therefore the church as a whole, to

- "receive the promised Spirit through faith" (3:14),
- "walk by the Spirit" (5:16; cf. 5:25),
- be "led by the Spirit" (5:18),
- bear "the fruit of the Spirit" (5:22–23), and
- "live by the Spirit" (5:25).

The life of the Christian and the church's life are impossible apart from the animating, helping, and beautifying work of the Spirit. In effect, Paul is telling the church of Galatia, "The standard is so enormously high that there's no possible way in our fallen state that we could ever attain the level of perfection and beauty adequate for the bride of Christ without the work of the Spirit."

The Greek term for "fruit" is *karpos*. While singular, it refers to the whole collection of spiritual fruit—love, joy, peace, patience, kindness, goodness, faithfulness, gentleness, self-control—occurring simultaneously in the Christian life. This fruit-blossoming, fruit-bearing, and fruit-maturing work of the Spirit in every believer's life results in an abundant harvest within the church. One cherry doesn't make a delicious cherry pie. It takes a harvest to produce a pie worth savoring. The fruit of the Spirit comes together to create a church that satisfies every taste bud of our Lord.

Love. This is not the butterflies-in-the-stomach, first-date kind of love or the tear-welling love at the reunion of friends. This is the sacrificial love that is conscious not of self-fulfillment but of self-giving. This kind of love is absolute in its resolve regardless of the response in return. Paul writes: "If I speak in the tongues of men and of angels, but have not love, I am a noisy gong or clanging cymbal. And if I have prophetic powers, and understand all mysteries and all knowledge, and if I have all faith, so as to remove mountains, but have not love, I am nothing" (1 Cor. 13:1–2). Even the celestial harmony of angelic ballads is nothing more than a child's kazoo compared with this selfless love. The Spirit beautifies the church by mirroring, through her members, the sacrificial love so graphically expressed in the death of Christ as we give and are given for the sake of others. Jesus doesn't simply have warm feelings toward us. Jesus has sacrificed himself on our behalf with a love that is freely given and flows out of a determined commitment to beautifying grotesque sinners. John expresses, "We love because he first loved us" (1 John 4:19). As a result of this undeserved love, we who believe willingly and lovingly give ourselves to his service by taking up our cross and worshipfuly presenting our "bodies as a living sacrifice, holy and acceptable to God" (Rom. 12:1). This measure of love within the body of Christ adorns and embellishes every facet of the church in a loveliness more beautiful than the voice of angels.

Joy. When the buds of joy blossom on the branch, the Spirit is generating more than mere happiness. The result is a "joy that is inexpressible and filled with glory" (1 Pet. 1:8). A joy unconditional, independent of the circumstances around us. Cultural demise? The church has joy. Political disorder? The church has joy. Worldwide pandemic? The church has joy. A joy that streams, without any circumstantial obstruction, out of a heart that is wholly satisfied in

Christ and the promises of Scripture. Foretelling his coming death, Jesus comforts his disciples:

> Truly, truly, I say to you, you will weep and lament, but the world will rejoice. You will be sorrowful, but your sorrow will turn to joy. When a woman is giving birth, she has sorrow because her hour has come, but when she has delivered the baby, she no longer remembers the anguish, for joy that a human being has been born into the world. So also you have sorrow now, but I will see you again, and your hearts will rejoice, and no one will take your joy from you. (John 16:20–22)

What reassuring words for his disciples, who didn't fully grasp what was about to occur and why it had to happen. Despite our varied life events, the Spirit gifts us with a joy that causes soul-stirring rejoicing even when all hope seems lost. The church should be the one glorious dwelling on earth that rejoices despite all that is happening outside her doors. The Spirit beautifies the church by anchoring her hope not in a kind of slap-happy giddiness so characteristic of worldly happiness, but in a joy founded on God himself, who is the fountain of all joy.

Peace. An incident in the life of Jesus reminds us of the type of peace birthed and fostered in the church by the Spirit. Amid a violent storm upon the Sea of Galilee, the disciples discover Jesus asleep in the boat's stern. They react by accusing him of caring more for his sleep than for their lives. Mark tells us, "He awoke and rebuked the wind and said to the sea, 'Peace! Be still!' And the wind ceased, and there was a great calm" (Mark 4:39).

This type of commanding peace is the fruit of the Spirit. Despite the howling gale and the crashing waves against the hull of the boat, a great calm resides within the heart of Christ. This form of tranquil peace pillows our head amid the storms of life in the conscious assurance that our sovereign God is the controller of every infinitesimal detail and is working all things for our good and his ultimate glory (Rom. 8:28). The Spirit beautifies the church by reminding her again and again of eternal truth revealed in Scripture. This settled truth peacefully anchors her into the safe harbor of God's promises in Christ, which "find their Yes in him" (2 Cor. 1:20).

Patience. This fruit is increasingly rare in the church. We exercise little patience with those who disagree with us. We extend little patience with those we disagree with. The Spirit beautifies the bride of Christ by producing within her self-restraint that doesn't retaliate. You may be more familiar with the word *long-suffering*, which denotes taking everything thrown at us, accepting it, and moving on. This fruit matures as it is incessantly nourished from the root of love (1 Cor. 13:4). It never seeks revenge for wrongs done. It faces ever-arduous situations. It always endures. In a season when retaliation and revenge fuel our daily interactions with others, the Spirit creates an atmosphere within the church that restrains our desire to lash out in vengeance and chains the beast of self-exaltation. The church is beautiful when she is a shining example of how to interact and respond to others in a manner that images forth Christ.

Kindness. The ministry of Christ is continually stamped with a posture of kindness—tender, gentle, genuine concern for others. Touching lepers, eating with tax collectors, healing beggars—Jesus's compassion has no bounds. Paul urges believers to "put on then, as God's chosen ones, holy and beloved, compassionate hearts, kindness, humility, meekness, and patience" (Col. 3:12).

Increasingly, the fruit of kindness is absent at the core of the body of Christ. Disagreements, dissension, and discord seem to mark today's church more than the fruit of kindness. Everyone is out for himself, her own ideas, their agendas. But the Spirit desires to beautify the church by creating succulent fruit on the branch that yields the sweetness of our tender care for fellow believers and unbelievers alike, those inside the church and those outside.

Goodness. The fruit of goodness conveys a determined resolve that all our actions and responses toward others will be made in light of living *coram Deo*, in the presence of God. The Old Testament emphasizes that "goodness" is an attribute of God (Neh. 9:25). Regardless of the need for confrontation with wayward creatures, God consistently acts out of his infinite goodness in a manner that brings ultimate glory to himself. There's nothing in God that pronounces a "got you now" or "you just watch out" disposition toward his children. God's goodness goes all the way to the blood-soaked cross in the place of hell-deserving sinners. The Spirit manifests this same attitude of goodness within the church, causing her people to go the extra mile to rescue others. In rejoicing, rebuke, exhortation, even in times of discipline, goodness toward wayward brothers and sisters keeps us beautifully demonstrating to every spectator that there are no perfect people—there is only a perfect Savior.

Faithfulness. Just the mention of this word brings to our remembrance the promise of Lamentations 3:22–23:

The steadfast love of the LORD never ceases;
  his mercies never come to an end;
they are new every morning;
  great is your faithfulness.

Our Lord's steadfast faithfulness is a reminder that he is unfailingly loyal to his people. He doesn't leave us to fend for ourselves, or figure it out ourselves, or even to pull ourselves up by our proverbial boot-straps. He doesn't leave his church without a commission, without equipping, or even without instructions. He is faithful to provide all we need for life and godliness. The same must be said of the bride of Christ: "It is required of stewards that they be found faithful" (1 Cor. 4:2). Faithful to obey Scripture. Faithful to advance Christ's kingdom. Faithful to equip the saints for the work of ministry. Faithful to love our neighbors. Faithful to exhibit patience, kindness, and goodness to others. Faithfulness is a work of the Holy Spirit (Acts 6:5). He beautifies the church through the fruit of faithfulness exhibited in her commitment and loyalty in serving others through Christ.

Gentleness. This fruit has been called "meekness" and speaks of a gentle blowing breeze that hints at strength but holds back in power. Anyone who lives on the coast will experience such a breeze. One minute it can be gentle and pleasant, and the next it can churn the waves, tossing sea spray into the air. This fruit also alludes to a tame beast with the strength to tear the flesh of a foe but the restraint not to unleash that strength.

Gentleness is a potency controlled by a humble heart. We recall the meekness of Jesus, who abandoned all heavenly privileges for a state of utter humility in the rubbish of this world. Gentleness, like the other fruit of the Spirit, is not a natural inclination. Our natural tendency is to power forth and tear through our opponents. Paul gives Timothy the command "But as for you, O man of God. . . . Pursue . . . gentle-ness" (1 Tim. 6:11). Gentleness is something we pursue. Again, in Colossians 3:12 Paul says, "Put on . . . meekness." Like our Christian armor, gentleness is something we must consciously put on every day.

The Spirit beautifies the church by gracing her with restrained strength. This isn't cowardice but is debased humility that keeps its power in check. It is one of the great mysteries of the church. Through the Spirit, she can turn the world upside down through controlled humility.

Self-control. How utterly miserable we are at keeping our actions, minds, and hearts in check. How vitally necessary it is that the Holy Spirit grow this fruit upon the branches of our hearts. Jesus, whose is the "same yesterday and today and forever," is the example we must follow (Heb. 13:8).

Self-control is not a fruit that believers may nibble. To be self-controlled is a command—a command to submit to the will of God at all times, in all circumstances, abandoning our selfish desires and sinful pleasures. Peter says, "Make every effort to supplement your faith with virtue, and virtue with knowledge, and knowledge with self-control, and self-control with steadfastness, and steadfastness with godliness, and godliness with brotherly affection, and brotherly affection with love" (2 Pet. 1:5–7). Self-control is hard work and effort. The Spirit beautifies the church by demonstrating through her that self-denial is our King's mandate. Our selves and wills are subservient to him—always.

———

Paul adds, "Against such things there is no law" (Gal. 5:23). The law doesn't beautify; it only reveals how filthy we are. When we adorn ourselves in the law, we choose to wear a wedding gown smeared in mud. But to be adorned in the beauty of the Spirit is to be spotless, clean, and beautiful—ready to meet our bridegroom.

Christ sent the Holy Spirit to be both Helper and beautifier of the church. Fully deserving of our worship, the Spirit accomplishes a work in each believer, and thereby in the body of Christ, that should be recognized as tantamount to the works of both the Father and the

Son. Thomas Goodwin wrote, "There is a general omission in the saints of God, in their not giving the Holy Ghost that glory that is due to his person. . . . The work he doth for us in its kinds is as great as those of the Father or the Son."[5] The church receives the full attention and beautifying work of every person of the Trinity. We have a Father and friend, a Savior and head, and a Helper and beautifier.

Let us ask ourselves, "If God is for us, who can be against us?" (Rom. 8:31).

---

5   Thomas Goodwin, *The Work of the Holy Ghost in Our Salvation*, in *The Works of Thomas Goodwin, D.D.*, ed. Thomas Smith, vol. 6 (1863; repr., Grand Rapids, MI: Reformation Heritage, 2006), 3.

6

A Pillar and Buttress of Truth

. . . a pillar and buttress of the truth.

I TIMOTHY 3:15

IN HER 1865 BOOK *Hans Brinker*, American author Mary Mapes Dodge chronicles the heroic story of the "little Dutch boy" who saves his country from catastrophic flooding by plugging his finger into a leaking dike. When the boy recognizes the imminent danger of a potentially broken dike and the destruction that will occur if a small trickle of water is allowed to slowly break away into a more considerable inundation, he flies into action. The story goes: "Quick as a flash, he saw his duty. Throwing away his flowers, the boy clambered up the heights until he reached the hold. His chubby little finger was thrust in, almost before he knew it. The flowing was stopped!"[1]

What can we do when the lies of this present age spring a leak in the church, which is supposed to hold back the torrent of the world's scheming deception? Some within the church would like to run for

---

1 Mary Mapes Dodge, *Hands Brinker; or The Silver Skates* (New York: Scribner, Armstrong, 1874), 134.

higher ground, cloistering themselves away from this growing danger. Others consider themselves impervious to the peril and rush to swim in the streams of the world, thinking they will never be polluted, only to end up drowning in the rushing waters of compromise. Still others, quite sincerely, just don't know how to respond.

Twisted Truth

With every passing day, and in seemingly greater frequency, the world not only is ambivalent to the truth of Scripture but hates the truth. The very concept of truth elicits severe mockery in favor of lies, half-truths, and the arrogant claim "I will decide what my truth is!" This subtle deception stems directly from the shrewd serpent and enemy of the bride of Christ, who began twisting the truth in the very beginning with his question to Eve, "Did God actually say . . . ?" (Gen. 3:1).

Twisting God's truth, Satan is cunning and crafty in chiseling away at the dike that holds his lies at bay. His duplicity plays out in three stages. First, the devil casts doubt on God's words. We see evidence of this in the question he asks Eve, "Did God *actually say*?" Second, Satan casts doubt on God's goodness. Eve soon falls prey to his trickery and starts to question the kindness and benevolence of God toward her and her husband, believing God has withheld vital happiness from them (Gen. 3:2–3). Third, this forked-tongued dragon convinces Eve to doubt God's authority by contradicting God's words. The serpent tells Eve that while God may have said she will die, "you will not surely die . . . [but] your eyes will be opened" (Gen. 3:4–5). Satan's objective is always the same, both in believers and in the church—to convince you to doubt God's words, doubt God's goodness, and doubt God's authority.

Satan hates you.

Satan hates the church.

Throughout the millennia since his fall, Satan has not altered his strategy of deceit. He has inundated every societal level with confusion and falsehood, from government, educational systems, mass media, and the family, to even the church. Through lies and half-truths, he convinces the world, for instance, that life begins at birth and not at conception; that the unborn child is a mere clump of cells to be eradicated with no moral implications; that life springs forth and evolves from nonliving coincidence, eliminating the need for a Creator; that true happiness is found within yourself; that your gender is a choice and not a gift; that eternal life is the result of many paths, all leading in the same direction—and the list could go on. Satan desires you to eat the deadly fruit of his twisted truth.

Paul warned the church at Corinth, "I am afraid that as the serpent deceived Eve by his cunning, your thoughts will be led astray from a sincere and pure devotion to Christ" (2 Cor. 11:3). Satan delights in leading the church away from faithful obedience to God and his word by inviting her members to swim and frolic in the waters of worldly lies. Unless we are held captive by God's word, the very heart of the church is susceptible to Satan's cunning deception. This is why, surrounded by a world of lies, the church must be ready to plug this leaking dike with God's truth.

Upholding Truth

In his magnificent hymn "The Church's One Foundation," Samuel J. Stone wrote:

> The Church's one foundation
> Is Jesus Christ, her Lord;
> She is His new creation
> By water and the Word:

From heav'n He came and sought her
To be His holy bride;
With His own blood He bought her,
And for her life He died.[2]

These melodic words remind us of Paul's description of the church to young Timothy as the "pillar and buttress of the truth" (1 Tim. 3:15). That's a vivid way of saying that it's the church's task to *uphold* the truth.

The Greek word for "buttress" is *hedraiōma* and means "support." This is the only time this word appears in the New Testament, and it defines the church as a bulwark of God's truth. The truth is her mission. The truth is her message. The truth is her reason for existing in the world.

On April 15, 2019, people worldwide were glued to their televisions and social media as the roof of Notre-Dame de Paris cathedral erupted in flames. The cathedral's spire snapped in two like a twig just before the sun set over the "City of Lights" crashing 314 feet into the nave, through the ceiling that skilled artisans had carved by hand in the Middle Ages, using five thousand oak trees. During the blaze, there was much speculation as to whether Notre Dame's twenty-eight flying buttresses—an invention of Gothic architecture—would collapse inward and bring down the building. Fortunately, they did not collapse, but it was a reminder to everyone watching that these buttresses, constructed in 1180, were the reason the structure has stood so long.[3] Without them, the whole edifice would have cascaded to the ground like matchsticks.

---

2 S. J. Stone, "The Church's One Foundation," 1866.
3 "Inside the Fight over How to Rebuild Notre Dame after Fire," *Time* (website), July 25, 2019, https://time.com/5634240/notre-dame-fire-france-battle/.

In Paul's meticulous description of Christ's church, he is saying to Timothy that once God's truth is removed from the church, her humanly devised structures, programs, and purpose for existing will collapse.

Bearing Witness to the Truth

During the final moments of his life, standing before Pontius Pilate, Jesus declared that the reason he came into the world was to "bear witness to the truth." He added, "Everyone who is of the truth listens to my voice" (John 18:37). Notice in his stunning testimony that Jesus proclaimed that he came to bear witness to *the* truth—not a vague, obscure, nebulous, open-to-one's-own-interpretation kind of truth. Jesus came to bear witness to only one truth, God's truth, the only truth that exists. The only truth that will still be standing when heaven and earth pass away (Matt. 24:35).

Jesus is the full and definitive expression of God's absolute truth (Heb. 1:1–4). His whole ministry fulfilled the divine charge of truth-bearer. It was prophesied that Jesus would be "full of . . . truth" (John 1:14). He called himself "the truth" (John 14:6). The entirety of Jesus's teaching and preaching ministry was characterized as "the way of God truthfully" (Matt. 22:16).

Jesus entered this lie-filled world, punching holes in the darkness with truth. He proclaimed the truth, pointed to the truth, bore witness to the truth, and confirmed the truth among all those who listened to his voice.

Pilate responded to Jesus's confession with the rhetorical "What is truth?" (John 18:38). Notice Pilate's omission of the definite article *the* before "truth." Some have considered this omission insignificant. But it's quite apparent that Pilate was purposefully placing truth into a relative framework. He perfectly epitomized the worldly skeptic who believes that truth does not exist in absolute categories but is merely left to one's private interpretation and personal circumstances. In contrast, the words of our Lord affirm that absolute truth—God's truth revealed in the Bible—exists and is the powerful reality to which his entire life bore witness.

The truth of which Jesus testified was handed down to Paul and, in turn, to Timothy, his brother and son in the faith (2 Tim. 1:2). Timothy had been one of Paul's longtime companions, who joined him on his second missionary journey (Acts 16:2), and who had been with Paul since the end of the apostle's first Roman imprisonment (Phil. 2:19–24). In many aspects, 2 Timothy serves as Paul's final words and is therefore vitally important as his final charge to his young disciple.

In 2 Timothy 3, Timothy is warned of the widespread "times of difficulty" that will plague the church in the days leading to the return of Christ (v. 1). These times, filled with those who oppose the truth, will be a constant reminder of the necessity to proclaim the truth of God. This truth, Paul emphasizes, is the sole authority upon which the church stands, serving as the means through which she battles the ideologies and treachery of the world. Since God's authority is bound up in Scripture, preaching, teaching, and proclaiming his truth unleashes his authoritative power over the "the prince of the power of the air, the spirit that is now at work in the sons of disobedience" (Eph. 2:2). Surrounded by sinful disobedience, Paul implores the church to depend wholly upon the word of God, for it is an entirely sufficient instrument through which the church will accomplish all her ministry.

All Scripture

The truth meant to be heralded by the church is found in a book. Paul identifies that book in 2 Timothy 3:16: "All Scripture is breathed out by God and profitable for teaching, for reproof, for correction, and for training in righteousness."

God's purpose is not merely to convey information to us—though he certainly accomplishes that. Through Scripture, God's purpose is to achieve for us more than can be achieved with uninspired human language. He conveys not only intellectual information but also tone, emotion, heart, and perspective. God's divine words are infinitely more beautiful than the words of men because through them, he conveys his character, purpose, power, plan, and mysterious glory. Employing a wide variety of writers with diverse backgrounds, cultures, methods, and vocabulary, God composes a final result that is precisely what he desires to communicate to his church.

The church affirms that the Bible is the product of "plenary inspiration," meaning that we are not allowed to pick and choose what we consider divine and what we consider human because all Scripture is, at the same time, divine and human. One of the issues that necessitated the seventeenth-century Protestant Reformation was the biblical conviction that the words of popes, churches, church councils, and other magisterial organizations do not possess the same authority as Scripture. While God used men to write his words, they remained his words—perfectly preserved, precisely inspired, absolutely sufficient.

We recall Peter's question to Jesus: "Lord, to whom shall we go? You have the words of eternal life" (John 6:68). The text of Scripture has no less authority than the divine voice of God. Though the words may come from the pen of David or Moses or Luke or Paul—different men in different eras writing in different styles—they are all God's divine words.

Breathed Out

All Scripture is "breathed out by God" (2 Tim. 3:16). This conveys something even more amazingly splendid. Consider your breath. It's something quite soft and intimate. Stand in a roaring crowd of sports fans, and you'll quickly discover just how soft your voice is when compared with the combined roar of everyone else. At the moment of birth, when a child gasps for that first breath of air, it's exhaled in return with the baby's first cry. Breathing is a sign of life. So too, God's breath is a giving of God's life.

The "breath of God" is a theme that can be traced throughout Scripture. In Genesis 1, God magnificently creates all things "according to their kinds" and each "according to its kind." But when he creates man and woman, he says, "Let us make man in our image, after our likeness" (Gen. 1:26). How does God accomplish this? He breathes upon him. "Then the LORD God formed the man of dust from the ground and *breathed* into his nostrils the *breath* of life, and the man became a living creature" (Gen. 2:7). In this creative act, there's a connection between the *likeness* of God and the *breath* of God.

Recounting the journey of the Israelites through the Red Sea on dry ground as they escaped the clutches of slavery in Egypt, 2 Samuel 22:16 says,

> Then the channels of the sea were seen;
>> the foundations of the world were laid bare,
> at the rebuke of the LORD,
>> at the blast of the *breath* of his nostrils.

In this act of deliverance, an association is made between the omnipotent power of God in parting the Red Sea and the *breath* of God.

The psalmist, reflecting upon the creation event, similarly says,

> Then the channels of the sea were seen,
>> and the foundations of the world were laid bare

at your rebuke, O LORD,

    at the blast of the *breath* of your nostrils. (Ps. 18:15)

And

By the word of the LORD the heavens were made,

    and by the *breath* of his mouth all their host. (Ps. 33:6)

The psalmist draws together the creative act of God and the *breath* of God.

In Isaiah 11:4, the prophet says, "With the *breath* of his lips he shall kill the wicked." A close association is established between the judgment of God upon the wicked and the *breath* of God.

At Calvary, Jesus "*breathed* his last" (Mark 15:37, 39; Luke 23:46). The final breath of Jesus was a sign and seal that sin had been atoned for, Jesus's great work of redemption was accomplished, righteousness had been purchased, God's holy wrath was satisfied, and the veil separating us from God was torn in two. On the cross, we recognize an association between the salvation of God and the *breath* of God. When Jesus appeared to his disciples after his resurrection, he "*breathed* on them and said to them, 'Receive the Holy Spirit'" (John 20:22). Here again, we see the relationship between the gift of the Spirit and the *breath* of God.

Even in salvation, there's an association between life and breath. Regeneration is literally God breathing the eternal sweet air of salvation into the corpse of a fallen sinner (John 3:3–8). You see, all of the Christian life is powered and animated by the breath of God.

Paul doesn't say that the Bible is "breathed upon by God"; Scripture is "breathed out by God." God's word is God's breath. And this divine breath brings life to his church, molding and shaping us into the image of Christ, sanctifying and renewing our hearts, maturing our churches, and making them gloriously beautiful dwellings.

The truth given to us through Scripture is the pillar and buttress of the church, having the same authority, relevance, and sufficiency as God himself, for the Bible is his divine breath.

Be What You Are

How does the church proclaim the truth of Christ in an ever-deeper cesspool of lies? First, she must separate herself and boldly refuse to be conformed to this present world—she must be continually transformed into imitators of Christ (Rom. 12:2; 1 Cor. 11:1). Second, the church must proclaim the countercultural truth of God's word, in love, before a hostile and unbelieving world (Col. 4:2–6). We must not beat people over the head with a Bible but must lovingly herald every command, commendation, and condemnation of Scripture. Third, the church must develop discerning wisdom, bringing every outside word captive to the obedience of Christ (2 Cor. 10:5).

When the church separates herself, she is hated (Matt. 10:22), slandered (1 Cor. 4:13), and persecuted, possibly unto death (Matt. 24:9). But those who persevere to the end—loving God's truth, proclaiming God's truth, and living God's truth—will be saved (Matt. 24:13).

In Jesus's Sermon on the Mount, he lovingly gazes over the crowd of people, proclaiming, "You are the light of the world" (Matt. 5:14). We are lights not because we emit inherent light but because Jesus, who is the light of the world, dwells in us and shines out through us (John 8:12). Christ is the truth God has breathed out. Christ is the truth that buttresses the church. As he is the radiant reflection of his Father's glory, so all believers reflect the same radiance of Christ. The world, full of hate, lies, deception, murder, half-truth, and even death, is illuminated by this light. So be what you are—blazing lights in a world of lies.

Once the little Dutch boy had plugged the leak that threatened his whole country, he thought, "with a boyish delight, the angry waters must stay back now! Haarlem shall not be drowned while I am here!" This should be the cry of every believer in Jesus Christ: "The world's lies and deceit must stay back now! My family, my church, my neighborhood, my country will not be drowned while I am here!" Do we love God's church to the extent that we will climb the highest peak to warn others of the impending threat to her beauty? The pillar and buttress of Scripture is the church's only hope when earthly ideological fires threaten to destroy all she holds dear. Read it. Love it. Proclaim it.

7

In Spirit and Truth

True worshipers will worship the Father in spirit and truth.

JOHN 4:23

THE EARLY CHURCH FATHER CYPRIAN said, "You can no longer have God for your Father, if you have not the Church for your mother."[1] Such a statement may sound strange to our modern sensibilities. Protestants may even muster a bit of nervousness as they hear in this statement the rattle of incense bowls and see the vestments of the priesthood. But John Calvin helps us with Cyprian's analogy to see that the church is vitally our "mother" in the sense that her ministry in our lives is essential in our Christian development and sanctification. For Calvin, we must

> learn even from the simple title "mother" how useful, indeed how necessary, it is that we should know her. For there is no other way to enter into life unless this mother conceive us in her womb, give us

---

1 Cyprian, *De catholica ecclesiae unitate* 6 (PL 4:503): "Habere jam non potest Deum patrem, qui Ecclesiam non habet matrem."

birth, nourish us at her breast, and lastly, unless she keep us under her care and guidance until, putting off mortal flesh, we become like the angels. Our weakness does not allow us to be dismissed from her school until we have been pupils all our lives. Furthermore, away from her bosom one cannot hope for any forgiveness of sins or any salvation.[2]

And

we must allow ourselves to be ruled and taught by men. This is the universal rule, which extends equally from the highest and the lowest. The church is the common mother of all the godly, which bears, nourishes, and brings up children to God, kings and peasants alike; this is done by the ministry. Those who neglect or despise this order choose to be wiser than Christ. Woe to the pride of such men![3]

Our "mother" is the church not of national or cultural identity but of spiritual sustenance as we humbly submit ourselves before God in beautiful worship.

The apex of our fellowship and communion with the Father, Son, and Holy Spirit is holy worship. Worship of God originates with God, not man. Worship was never the idea or plan of man, as there's nothing in us that seeks after God or even desires to know him (Rom. 3:11). The desire to worship God is wrought in the heart of believers by the Holy Spirit. We love God because he first loved us. We seek God because he first sought us. We worship God because he commands such worship, and we willingly obey.

---

2 John Calvin, *Institutes of the Christian Religion*, ed. John T. McNeill, trans. Ford Lewis Battles (Philadelphia: Westminster Press, 1960), 4.1.4. For a fuller treatment, see Jonathan Gibson and Mark Earngey, eds., *Reformation Worship* (Greensboro, NC: New Growth, 2018), 51.

3 John Calvin, *Commentaries on the Epistles of Paul to the Galatians and Ephesians*, trans. William Pringle (Edinburgh: Calvin Translation Society, 1854), 282.

The context in which worship is most abundantly realized is within the church—not ornate buildings, entertaining experiences, or worship liturgies, but God's gathered people. Worship is the conscious recognition of God's sovereign greatness and resplendent, holy beauty and our ascribing honor, adoration, reverence, and glory to him. It is the bride of Christ extolling praise and adoration to who God is, what he has done, and what he has promised to do. It is the forsaking of all idols in our lives—which divert our focus, attention, and devotion—and singularly riveting our hearts and minds on the supreme, transcendent God of the cosmos.

You may have thought worship had to do with a dynamic music program, a passionate praise band, or a robed reverential choir. Nothing could be further from biblical reality. While forms of worship are essential, these in and of themselves are not worship. Legitimate worship consists of thinking, believing, and living for God's glory and honor.

Beautiful Worship

John Owen said that the church should regularly be finding ways to express worship in manners that are "more decent, beautiful, and orderly."[4] What did Owen mean by "beautiful" worship? Was this beauty meant to proceed from rites and rituals, incense and candles, worship bands and spotlights? Was he talking about organizing a *worship experience* wherein the participant is caught up in a trance-like state in a darkened, fog-filled room? This is not quite what Owen

---

4 John Owen, *Brief Instruction*, in *The Works of John Owen*, ed. William H. Goold, 24 vols. (1850–1855; repr., vols. 1–16, Edinburgh: Banner of Truth, 1965–1968), 15:467. See Joel R. Beeke and Mark Jones, "John Owen on the Christian Sabbath and Worship," chap. 41 in *A Puritan Theology* (Grand Rapids, MI: Reformation Heritage, 2012), 653–79.

had in mind. For worship to be biblically beautiful, Owen believed, it must focus on the triune God.

> All acceptable devotion in them that worship God is the effect of faith, which respects the precepts and promises of God alone. And the comeliness and beauty of gospel worship consisteth in its relation unto God by Jesus Christ, as the merciful high priest over his house, with the glorious administration of the Spirit therein.[5]

We would do well to keep in mind that "God is spirit, and those who worship him must worship in spirit and truth" (John 4:24). This is the only manner of devotion and worship that God accepts. God seeks those who will worship "in spirit." The Greek is quite clear here. It does not say "in *the* Spirit" but "in spirit." Jesus is not instructing believers to worship in the Holy Spirit but *with* or *in* the human spirit. He is telling the Samaritan woman in John 4 not only that he desires worship that flows from a knowledge of the truth of who he is, but also that he is looking for worshipers who will worship from the very depth of their inner being—their spirit.

Authentic biblical worship occurs only when the very core of our being is employed in worshiping God. Our lips may mouth the words, our hands may be lifted upward, our eyes may fill with tears, but unless these expressions flow from "the effect of faith," as Owen describes, our worship is mere performance. Valid worship proceeds from the heart of faith, for "without faith it is impossible to please him, for whoever would draw near to God must believe that he exists and that he rewards those who seek him" (Heb. 11:6). Worship isn't born in the void of our conscience but proceeds from truth.

5 Owen, *Works*, 15:467.

The truth of who God is as revealed in his word, the understanding of who Christ is and what he accomplished in his incarnation, the realization of who the Spirit is and what he is currently doing in our lives. Without truth born in faith, worship becomes ordinary, humdrum, and even carnal.

In John 4:23, a peculiar phrase warrants our attention here: "The Father is seeking such people to worship him." Wait. Don't we, as worshipers, seek God? Indeed, we do. All genuine worship begins with a heartfelt seeking after God. This is the clarion call of 1 Chronicles 16:8–11:

> Oh give thanks to the LORD; call upon his name;
> make known his deeds among the peoples!
> Sing to him, sing praises to him;
> tell of all his wondrous works!
> Glory in his holy name;
> let the hearts of those who seek the LORD rejoice!
> Seek the LORD and his strength;
> seek his presence continually!

Extended to all believers, the command is clear: "seek his presence continually." But Jesus reminds his people not only that we seek God in worship but also that he is seeking us. The Father is actively pursuing those whose hearts yearn to bask in his omnipotent glory.

It's easy to fall into the trap of the conventionally humdrum "worship service," giving little thought to the extemporaneous beauty that becomes a reality when we properly behold the holiness of God. We don't have to work up some frenzied performance to appease God; we just need to come in faith and truth offering our innermost selves, for God is already pursuing and singing over us (Zeph. 3:17).

Gospel Simplicity

Gospel-shaped worship is beautiful when it flows from a mind informed by truth and a heart willing to abandon all for the sake of communion with God. Reading about the Old Testament's worship practices, we might easily stand in awe of the ornaments encased in pure gold, the rare jewels adorning the chest of the high priest, and the countless burnt sacrifices offered as an aroma before God. Chapter after chapter details instructions for building, embellishing, and beautifying the house of worship. When we arrive at the New Testament, a gospel simplicity replaces all the outward rites and ceremonies of the law. Paul says in 2 Corinthians 3:7–11:

> Now if the ministry of death, carved in letters on stone, came with such glory that the Israelites could not gaze at Moses' face because of its glory, which was being brought to an end, will not the ministry of the Spirit have even more glory? For if there was glory in the ministry of condemnation, the ministry of righteousness must far exceed it in glory. Indeed, in this case, what once had glory has come to have no glory at all, because of the glory that surpasses it. For if what was being brought to an end came with glory, much more will what is permanent have glory.

The reflecting glory on Moses's face was a fading and passing glory, signifying the impermanence of the old covenant. The glory in this system was not the full reality of God's plan but acted as a shadow of what was to come—something permanent, eternally glorious, and eminently more beautiful. The *glory* of worship consists not in the "pompous observance of outward ceremonies" but exclusively in Jesus Christ, who is better than anything previously offered.[6]

---

6 Owen, *Works*, 15:469.

The gospel simplicity that replaces ceremonialist performance is the message of salvation through faith in God's final Word to man—Jesus Christ. He is infinitely more beautiful than gold or jewels. Christ's sacrificial death on the cross has obtained "an eternal redemption" for his people (Heb. 9:12), making him "the mediator of a new covenant" (Heb. 9:15). Before, there was trepidation; now there is boldness. Before, there was slavery; now there is liberty. Before, there was complexity; now there is simplicity.

Worshipers are now free to come before the throne of grace, by-passing the folderol of the old way, now having access to a better way, for "through him we both have access in one Spirit to the Father. So then you are no longer strangers and aliens, but you are now fellow citizens with the saints and members of the household of God" (Eph. 2:18–19).

The writer of Hebrews fittingly captures how worshipers are now allowed to enter behind the veil: "Therefore, brothers, since we have confidence to enter the holy places by the blood of Jesus, by the new and living way that he opened for us through the curtain, that is, through his flesh, and since we have a great high priest over the house of God . . ." (Heb. 10:19–21). Concerning these verses, Owen comments, "This is the glory of gospel worship and the beauty of it; whose consideration whilst the minds of men are diverted from, to look for beauty in the outward preparation of ceremonies, they lose the privilege purchased for believers by the blood of Christ."[7]

The beauty of gospel worship, the worship with which we must concern ourselves as the bride of Christ, is found not in ritual and ceremony but in Christ and Christ alone. There is no glory in any

7 Owen, *Works*, 15:469.

other worship than the worship that comes by and is exclusively in Jesus Christ. For in him, the beauty of worship consists and becomes simple, spiritual, and heavenly.

Corporate Worship

In an age of "worship wars," it would be incumbent upon the church to reexamine the mandate, mode, and method of worship. For the past several decades, worship seems to have taken on a predominantly individual rather than corporate emphasis. Various references could be offered to substantiate the scriptural teaching that worship is to be practiced in private. For instance, Jesus commanded individual worship when he instructed each of us to go into his or her prayer closet and shut the door, assuring us that "your Father who sees in *secret* will reward you" (Matt. 6:6). Perhaps this is even what Joshua had in mind when he vowed, "As for me and *my house*, we will serve the LORD" (Josh. 24:15).

However, worship in the New Testament is viewed predominantly in a corporate setting. It was Jesus's custom each Sabbath day to go into a synagogue and join with others in the reading of Scripture (Luke 4:16). The author of Hebrews admonishes his readers not to forsake the assembling of themselves together (Heb. 10:25). Corporate worship was not merely a suggestion in Scripture but a command. When God's people meet together, we enter into the place where God dwells—God meets with us, and we meet with God. Through Christ, we find ourselves face-to-face before God himself. If the church were fully conscious of that sumptuous truth, what beauty and loveliness would characterize our corporate worship! Perhaps we would exclaim with Jacob at Bethel: "How awesome is this place! This is none other than the house of God, and this is the gate of heaven" (Gen. 28:17). Or with John, on the island of Patmos, we would together behold in the midst of the lampstands one like a son of man, clothed with a long robe with a golden sash around his chest. The hairs of his head were white, like white wool, like snow. His eyes were like a flame of fire, his feet were like burnished bronze, refined in a furnace, and his voice was like the roar of many waters. In his right hand he held seven stars, and from his mouth came a sharp two-edged sword, and his face was like the sun shining in full strength. (Rev. 1:13–16)

For this mode of worship to be a present reality within the church, our methods must mirror those of Scripture—reading of Scripture; preaching and exhortation from the word; offering of prayers, hymns, and spiritual songs; confession of sin; celebration of the ordinances; practicing the ordinary means of grace; giving gifts; fellowship among believers—all with a beautiful, holy fear and reverence that our God has sought such worshipers. What wonder and glory that God meets with his church, that they are his people, and that he is their God.

8

Shepherding the Flock

Shepherd the flock of God that is among you.

I PETER 5:2

FAITHFUL LEADERS BEAUTIFY THE CHURCH.

The undershepherds of the flock of God beautify the church through their godly lives, faithful work, biblical leadership, and dedicated service. The purpose of this chapter isn't to present a case for a particular type of church government or to present a denominational framework of leadership. This chapter is about how the church's leaders aid in the bride's beautification and how the church becomes all the more radiant because of their service to and through her.

Some churches view their governance as though the church were a business, with a chief executive officer to rule over their congregation. Others want entrepreneurs who are continually innovating because they think numerical growth comes through clever techniques. However, these worldly leadership models nowhere resemble the biblical pattern of leadership within the body of Christ. Biblical offices are incomparable with management of earthly organizations because they have the utmost honor of representing the Lord Jesus Christ, the church's supreme head.

Faithful leaders beautify the church when they recognize that they are mere representatives of Christ and subordinate to him in all things. In other words, any authority these governing servants possess is a delegated authority from their sovereign head. When Jesus commissioned and sent out his disciples, he said, "All authority in heaven and on earth has been given to *me*. . . . And behold, *I am* with you always, to the end of the age" (Matt. 28:18, 20). Any authority leaders within the church retain is Christ's authority. That vicarious authority promises that he will be with us, working in and through us to exercise such jurisdiction in the love and care of his bride. After his resurrection, when Jesus appeared to his disciples, he assured them, "As the Father has sent me, even so I am sending you" (John 20:21). Jesus calls. Jesus commissions. Jesus sends. The church belongs to him.

The apostle Paul begins almost all of his epistles by reminding his readers that he is a subordinate servant of Christ:

- "Paul, a servant of Christ Jesus" (Rom. 1:1).
- "Paul, an apostle of Christ Jesus" (2 Cor. 1:1).
- "Paul, an apostle . . . through Jesus Christ" (Gal. 1:1).
- "Paul, an apostle of Christ Jesus" (Eph. 1:1).
- "Paul and Timothy, servants of Christ Jesus" (Phil. 1:1).
- "Paul, an apostle of Christ Jesus" (Col. 1:1).
- "Paul, an apostle of Christ Jesus" (1 Tim. 1:1).
- "Paul, an apostle of Christ Jesus" (2 Tim. 1:1).
- "Paul, a servant of God and an apostle of Jesus Christ" (Titus 1:1).
- "Paul, a prisoner for Christ Jesus" (Philem. 1:1).

You get the picture. Peter, James, and Jude were no different in how they opened their epistles.

When leaders within the church admit and demonstrate that they are subservient to Christ, all other ministries within the church display a rare beauty that shines with the glory of Christ. In short, the church isn't a man-centered, egotistical spectacle but is a Christ-exalting organism led by gospel-driven servanthood. All who desire to make the church beautiful adopt as their life motto "Not from men nor through man, but through Jesus Christ" (Gal. 1:1).

The Ministry of a Pastor

Scripture is clear that the primary position of leadership and care within the body of Christ is the position of pastor. This office is known by many titles used interchangeably throughout the New Testament. Below are five biblical titles given to this one office:

1. *Elder* (*presbyteros*): someone tasked with the administration and spiritual guidance of the church. He has been set over the congregation. He is a steward of God, a manager of God's household who administers the spiritual treasures of God's mysteries (1 Cor. 4:1; 1 Thess. 5:12; 1 Tim. 5:17; Titus 1:7).

2. *Bishop* or *overseer* (*episkopos*): one who exercises the function of overseeing. In the areas of teaching, he is a general superintendent over the spiritual well-being of the flock (1 Thess. 5:12; 1 Tim. 5:17; Titus 1:9; 1 Pet. 5:2).

3. *Shepherd* or *pastor* (*poimēn*): a presiding officer of an assembly. He is one who has committed himself to the care of others by watching over, defending, and loving the sheep of God's flock (Acts 20:28–31; Eph. 4:11).

4. *Preacher* (*kēryx*): a herald or messenger vested with the authority to proclaim the truth by teaching and preaching God's word (Rom. 10:14; 1 Tim. 2:7; 2 Tim. 1:11).

5. *Teacher* (*didaskalos*): one who teaches both the things of God and the duties of man for the purpose of edification, instruction, and correction (1 Cor. 12:28–29; 1 Tim. 2:7).

It's evident that a pastor's role is singularly bound up with the varied duties of elder, overseer, shepherd, preacher, and teacher, all of which serve to care for, guide, instruct, and watch over the flock of God.

To serve in this role or office, one must meet a high standard. Each man of God needs to endure a time of testing or proving to be placed in such a lofty position of shepherding oversight. This period of testing uncovers the qualifications that must be characteristic of all undershepherds of the household of God. First Timothy 3:2–3 lists ten such qualifications:

- "the husband of one wife"
- "sober-minded"
- "self-controlled"
- "respectable"
- "hospitable" to others
- "able to teach" God's word
- "not a drunkard"
- "not violent but gentle"
- "not quarrelsome"
- "not a lover of money"

The proving grounds for each qualification are three separate spheres of influence: his home and family (vv. 4–5), his spiritual maturity (v. 6), and his community (v. 7). Within these three contexts, this man's character is continually and consistently scrutinized and proven. When men are placed into a pastoral role without having met these qualifications, immeasurable harm befalls the church.

Churches radiate the beauty of Christ only when they are faithful to appoint men who themselves are beautiful in character and holiness. We all have heard and read devastating stories of churches that lose all credibility and destroy their witness because they appoint men to leadership positions who fail to meet the above qualifications. That is not to say that churches must find perfect men to serve. There are no sinless leaders. Instead, the church needs to find men who, through proper testing and refining, demonstrate that they meet the biblical injunction and qualifications to serve.

Martin Bucer, a disciple of the magisterial Reformer Martin Luther and teacher of John Calvin, was called the "Pastoral Theologian of the Reformation" because of his extensive meditation and teaching on the pastoral role within the church. In his *De Regno Christi*, Bucer identifies three duties of a pastor: (1) to diligently teach the Holy Scriptures, (2) to administer the sacraments, and (3) to participate in the discipline of the church. The third has three parts: life and manners, penance (involving severe sin), and sacred ceremonies (worship and fasting). A fourth duty is to care for the needy.[1] Bucer wrote:

> Those pastors and teachers of the churches who want to fulfill their office and keep themselves clean of the blood of those of their flocks who are perishing should not only publicly administer Christian doctrine but also announce, teach and entreat repentance toward God and faith in our Lord Jesus Christ, and whatever contributes toward piety, among all who do not reject this doctrine of

---

1 Martin Bucer, *"De Regno Christi,"* in *Melanchthon and Bucer*, ed. Wilhelm Pauck (London: SCM, 1969), 232–59. See also James F. Stitzinger, "Pastoral Ministry in History," in *Rediscovering Pastoral Ministry*, ed. John MacArthur (Nashville: W Publication Group, 1995), 34–63.

salvation, even at home and with each one privately. . . . For the faithful ministers of Christ should imitate this their master and chief shepherd of the churches, and seek most lovely themselves whatever has been lost, including the hundredth sheep wandering from the fold, leaving behind the ninety-nine which remain in the Lord's fold (Matt. 18:12).[2]

To be a biblically faithful pastor and faithfully beautify the church, one's heart must beat in rhythm with the heart of Christ, both privately and publicly. There is no room for error in doctrine or failure in holiness.

Bucer's work *Concerning the True Care of Souls* is perhaps his most thorough analysis of pastoral ministry. There he says:

From this it is evident that there are five main tasks required in the pastoral office and true care of souls. First: to lead to Christ our Lord and into his communion those who are still estranged from him, whether through carnal excess or false worship. Secondly: to restore those who had once been brought to Christ and into his church but have been drawn away again through the affairs of the flesh or false doctrine. Thirdly: to assist in the true reformation of those who while remaining in the church of Christ have grievously fallen and sinned. Fourthly: to re-establish in true Christian strength and health those who, while persevering in the fellowship of Christ and not doing anything particularly or grossly wrong, have become somewhat feeble and sick in the Christian life. Fifthly: to protect from all offense and falling away and continually encourage in all good things those who stay within the flock and in

2 Bucer, *"De Regno Christi,"* 235.

Christ's sheep-pen without grievously sinning or becoming weak and sick in their Christian walk.[3]

Evident within Bucer's words is that pastoral ministry principally involves a focus upon those to whom we minister. Ministry isn't beautiful because of the pastors' cunning administrative skills, his creative genius in program development, or even his larger-than-life personality. The pastoral ministry beautifies the church only when it looks beyond all the ego-boosting devices within ministry and beholds helpless lambs.

Men often enter pastoral ministry because of their ardent love for Christ, the chief shepherd, but quickly discover that their love isn't as robust for his sheep, who are often stubborn animals. Such men may face immediate opposition, difficulty, and dissent from obstinate church members, causing such pastors to question their calling and sometimes even leading them to drop out of ministry altogether. Sadly, pastors too often say, "I would love the ministry if it weren't for the people." Pastors become disheartened, hardened, and desensitized, losing the zeal they used to possess. As a result, they retreat into their study desiring to protect themselves from heartache while neglecting the needs of the people of whom they've been given charge.

If we are to recommit ourselves to the beauty and loveliness of the church, we must recognize that people are the ministry. As tricky and difficult as they may sometimes be, Jesus is our supreme example of love extended to wayward sinners. The ministry consists of searching for the lost, strengthening the weak, comforting the grieving,

---

3   Martin Bucer, *Concerning the True Care of Souls*, trans. Peter Beale (Edinburgh: Banner of Truth, 2009), 70.

challenging the weary, restoring the fallen, and feeding the spiritually hungry. In other words, while vital in the life of the church, preaching is only part of the greater whole of pastoral ministry.

In his "Of the Calling of the Ministry," William Perkins describes the minister as, first, an *angel* or "Messenger of God"—that is, the "Messenger of the Lord of Hosts" to the people. Second, he is an *interpreter*—that is, "one who can deliver aright the reconciliation, made betwixt God and man." "Every minister is a double Interpreter, God's to the people and the people's to God."[4] To this, Perkins adds the necessity of being a "godly minister" and urges men to be dedicated to this high office.

> For the Physician's care for the body or the Lawyer's care of the cause, are both inferior duties to this of the Minister. A good Lawyer may be one of ten, a good Physician one of twenty, a good man one of 100, but a good Minister is one of 1000. A good Lawyer may declare the true state of thy cause, a Physician may declare the true state of the body: No calling, no man can declare unto thee thy righteousness, but a true minister.[5]

The type of pastor described in Scripture, Perkins admits, is a rare find. A church should always consider such a discovery a blessing from God and his desire to make the church beautiful. In every sphere of his responsibility—worshiping, preaching, modeling, leading, outreaching, discipling, watching, warning[6]—the pastor desires

---

4 William Perkins, *The Works of That Famous and Worthie Minister of Christ in the Universitie of Cambridge, M. W. Perkins*, 3 vols. (Cambridge, England: University of Cambridge, 1608–1609), 3:430–31.

5 Perkins, *Works*, 3:435–36.

6 See chaps. 14–20 in John F. MacArthur, *Pastoral Ministry: How to Shepherd Biblically* (Nashville: Thomas Nelson, 2005).

to exalt Christ, proclaim God's word, love his people, and thereby beautify the church.

Jonathan Edwards wrote:

> More especially is the uniting of a faithful minister with a particular Christian people as their pastor, when done in a due manner, like a young man marrying a virgin. . . .
>
> The minister joyfully devoting himself to the service of his Lord in the work of the ministry, as a work that he delights in, and also joyfully uniting himself to the society of the saints that he is set over . . . and they, on the other hand, joyfully receiving him as a precious gift of their ascended Redeemer.[7]

Pastors and churches who subscribe to this biblical pattern of leadership view the pastor as a "precious gift" from God and therefore should expect the same divine blessing experienced by the church in Acts: "And the word of God continued to increase, and the number of the disciples multiplied greatly" (Acts 6:7).

The Ministry of a Deacon

In addition to the office of pastor, another critical role within the life of the body is that of a deacon. While Scripture doesn't specifically detail a deacon's responsibilities within the church, it does emphasize the key qualification for such an office—moral character. The attention Scripture devotes to the moral integrity, spiritual maturity, and doctrinal purity of those who serve the body of Christ highlights the importance of holiness within the life of the church and how such holiness serves to beautify.

---

7 Jonathan Edwards, *The Works of Jonathan Edwards*, ed. Edward Hickman, 2 vols. (1834; repr., Edinburgh: Banner of Truth, 1974), 2:19–20.

While the diaconal office has been defined and explained in various ways, a deacon quite simply is a servant. Originally, the verb *diakoneō* may have meant "serve tables" (Acts 6:2). But more broadly, the noun *diakonos* came to represent those who give themselves to any service to meet the needs of the people. A deacon is, like the governing authorities, a "servant for your good" and a "servant of God" (Rom. 13:3–4).

John Owen recognized the foundation for the office of deacon in such passages as John 12:8, "For the poor you always have with you," and Deuteronomy 15:11: "For there will never cease to be poor in the land. Therefore I command you, 'You shall open wide your hand to your brother, to the needy and to the poor, in your land.'" Owen suggested that a deacon's work initially fell upon the apostles' shoulders as the first and only officers within the church.

Additionally, Owen saw deacons as servants of mercy who held no inherent authority, rule, or leadership within the church. Their singular purpose was providing help to others, thereby setting pastors free to dedicate themselves wholly to the ministry of the word.[8]

The traditional foundation of the calling of deacons to serve in the church is offered in Acts 6:1–6:

> Now in these days when the disciples were increasing in number, a complaint by the Hellenists arose against the Hebrews because their widows were being neglected in the daily distribution. And the twelve summoned the full number of the disciples and said, "It is not right that we should give up preaching the word of God to serve tables. Therefore, brothers, pick out from among you seven men of good repute, full of the Spirit and of wisdom,

---

8 Sinclair Ferguson, *John Owen on the Christian Life* (Edinburgh: Banner of Truth, 1987), 169.

whom we will appoint to this duty. But we will devote ourselves to prayer and to the ministry of the word." And what they said pleased the whole gathering, and they chose Stephen, a man full of faith and of the Holy Spirit, and Philip, and Prochorus, and Nicanor, and Timon, and Parmenas, and Nicolaus, a proselyte of Antioch. These they set before the apostles, and they prayed and laid their hands on them.

While this text demonstrates a specific need within the church, these seven established men, while perhaps not fulfilling the role as later developed in the New Testament, certainly anticipate the deacons' function.

In one sense, every member of a local congregation is a servant. Paul entreated the whole church to "serve one another" through love (Gal. 5:13). Jesus said that the one who serves is "greatest" in the kingdom (Mark 9:34–35). However, according to the Acts passage above, a deacon has a recognized role within the church in that faithful believers are identified and called out specifically for acts of service. This becomes all the more evident when we arrive in 1 Timothy 3:8–13 and read the list of qualifications for such an office. With qualifications similar to those of a pastor or elder, a deacon must be

- "dignified"
- "not double-tongued"
- "not addicted to much wine"
- "not greedy for dishonest gain"
- of "a clear conscience"
- faithful to "hold the mystery of the faith"
- "the husband of one wife"
- adept at "managing their children and their own households well"

There has been much debate regarding verse 11, "Their wives likewise must be dignified, not slanderers, but sober-minded, faithful in all things," and whether this verse has in view the wives of male deacons or women themselves serving in the office of deacon. Regardless, it's evident that a wife of a deacon can disqualify her husband from holding the office if she is undignified, slanderous, intemperate, and unfaithful. It's also unmistakable that the New Testament refers to women with the same Greek word—*diakonos*, meaning "servant"—as is used for "deacon." Phoebe, in Romans 16:1, provides such an example. Irrespective of your interpretation of the passage, it's apparent that a biblical servant's role is to beautify the church by demonstrating the mercy of Christ, who took upon himself the "form of a servant" (Phil. 2:7).

If we were to sum up a deacon's qualifications in a single phrase, it would be "full of the Spirit" (Acts 6:3; cf. Eph. 5:18). A deacon's moral character must be above reproach in all things. In public, deacons must prove exemplary in life, speech, integrity, and heart. In private, deacons must also evidence commitment to the truth of God's word and the holiness of their homes. By leading his family well, the deacon demonstrates that he can serve in key roles of responsibility within the church.

A deacon beautifies the church, first, by being a visible, unassuming, unadorned representative of the Lord Jesus Christ, who himself washed his disciples' dirty feet (John 13:1–13). Second, the deacon is a selfless servant to all. He doesn't pick and choose his favorite people to help. He willingly and sacrificially sets his desires aside to serve the widow, the hungry, the poor, the grieving, the helpless, and the sick alike. Third, the deacon emulates God, who is "Father of the fatherless and protector of widows" (Ps. 68:5). He helps "bring justice to the fatherless" and pleads "the widow's cause" (Isa. 1:17).

In short, his role is to include looking after "orphans and widows" (James 1:27). He helps beautify the church by caring for those who have no one else to care for them.

Christ, the supreme head of the church, doesn't leave us to grope about in darkness, trying to discover innovative ways to lead and help ourselves. He's dispensed all we need and administers his bride's authority, leadership, and care by assigning specific biblical offices to be his representatives on earth.

There's no greater calling or duty than to lead and serve the bride of Christ. It's not drudgery or burdensome, but delightful and lovely. Any church that doesn't subscribe to the biblical roles of pastor and deacon forfeits the biblical blessing of being beautiful in the sight of Christ, edifying to the people of God, and attractive to a sinful world. May Herman Bavinck's words ring forth as a blasting trumpet in every church that would call herself Christ's:

> All the ministrations and offices which Christ instituted into his church are centered in the Word. He gave his disciples no worldly power (Matt. 20:25–27), nor priestly lordship (1 Pet. 5:3), for they are all spiritual persons (1 Cor. 2:10–16), anointed by the Holy Spirit (1 John 2:20), and together forming a royal priesthood (1 Pet. 2:9). The endowments and the offices have only this end that those who receive them serve one another by means of them in love (Rom. 13:8; Gal. 5:13). The weapons of their warfare are purely spiritual in character (2 Cor. 10:4); they consist of the girdle of truth, the breastplate of righteousness, the shield of faith, the helm of salvation, and the sword of the Spirit (Eph. 6:14–17).[9]

---

9 Herman Bavinck, *The Wonderful Works of God* (Glenside, PA: Westminster Seminary Press, 2019), 521.

9

Feeding the Flock

Preach the word.

2 TIMOTHY 4:2

IF WE COULD SELECT only one text to describe pastoral ministry, it would be difficult to find a passage with more enormity than these words from Paul to Timothy:

> I charge you in the presence of God and of Christ Jesus, who is to judge the living and the dead, and by his appearing and his kingdom: preach the word; be ready in season and out of season; reprove, rebuke, and exhort, with complete patience and teaching. For the time is coming when people will not endure sound teaching, but having itching ears they will accumulate for themselves teachers to suit their own passions, and will turn away from listening to the truth and wander off into myths. As for you, always be sober-minded, endure suffering, do the work of an evangelist, fulfill your ministry. (2 Tim. 4:1–5)

We've already discussed the emotion 2 Timothy evokes when you realize this letter contains Paul's final words to his young disciple and son in the faith. His commission is direct, candid, and, we could even say, profoundly deliberate. Paul is basically saying, "Timothy, what I am about to tell you is said before God and Christ as my witness, the Judge of the world, to whose kingdom we belong, and before whom we will one day stand and give an account for our earthly ministry."

The Heart of Ministry

When we survey the "great preachers" throughout church history, we're often drawn to the Puritan age and the heartfelt tenderness of Thomas Goodwin, the deep reasoning of John Owen, the pastoral burden of Richard Sibbes, and the down-to-earth exposition of John Bunyan. The warp and woof of the Puritan era was that preaching and personal holiness were tightly woven together with genuine care for people.[1]

A beautiful illustration of biblical ministry appears in John Bunyan's timeless work *The Pilgrim's Progress*. Christian, the main character in this illustrious tale, sees a picture hanging on the wall when he comes into Interpreter's house. The man portrayed "had eyes lifted up to Heaven, the best books in his hand, the law of truth written upon his lips, the world behind his back. He stood as if pleading with men, and a crown of gold hung over his head." Interpreter describes what Christian sees:

> The man in this picture represents one of a thousand: he can conceive children, travail in birth with children, and nurse them himself when they are born. You see him with his eyes lifted up to Heaven, the best of books in his hand and the law of truth written on his lips. All this is to show you that his work is to know and

---

1 For more insight into the preaching of the Puritans, see Sinclair Ferguson, *Some Pastors and Teachers* (Edinburgh: Banner of Truth, 2017).

unfold dark things to sinners. You see him pleading with men, the world cast behind him, and a crown hanging over his head to show you that by rejecting and despising the things of this present world for the love that he has to his Master's service, he is sure to have glory as his reward in the world to come. . . . [This] is the only man authorized by the Lord of the place where you are going to be your guide in all difficult places you will encounter on the way.[2]

Every allegorical element of this portrait inhabits the heart of pastoral ministry—relentless devotion to Scripture, ardent affection for God's people, heavenly minded commitment to kingdom work, and prayerful dependency upon the Lord.

Our particular time in church history seems to have given rise to a profile that is anything but the above description. This is the age of the intellectual, the professor, the cultural commentator, the entertainer, and the para-church ministry leader. The role of the pastor has become quite secondary. Bunyan's description is absent in so many evangelical circles as men have abandoned their role as watchmen for a more comfortable seat on the fringe of ministry. Where are those who profess, "I behold the church, and she is beautiful!"

Pastoral Charge

In 2 Timothy 4, with sweeping brushstrokes, Paul paints his own picture of an undershepherd. Throughout this letter, he has been entrusting to Timothy a series of convicting ministry charges:

I remind you to fan into flame the gift of God, which is in you through the laying on of my hands. (2 Tim. 1:6)

2   John Bunyan, *The Pilgrim's Progress: From This World to That Which Is to Come*, ed. C. J. Lovik (Wheaton, IL: Crossway, 2009), 46–47.

Be strengthened by the grace that is in Christ Jesus, and what you have heard from me in the presence of many witnesses entrust to faithful men, who will be able to teach others also. (2 Tim. 2:1–2)

Do your best to present yourself to God as one approved, a worker who has no need to be ashamed, rightly handling the word of truth. (2 Tim. 2:15)

Flee youthful passions and pursue righteousness, faith, love, and peace, along with those who call on the Lord from a pure heart. (2 Tim. 2:22)

But as for you, continue in what you have learned and have firmly believed, knowing from whom you learned it. (2 Tim. 3:14)

And then he begins a final injunction,

I charge you. . . . (2 Tim. 4:1)

In Greek, this phrase is not composed of three words as in our English translation but is one strong word that expresses an earnest testimony, solemn command, and strong urging. Paul isn't offering suggestions here but is voicing a strong compulsion for fervent ministry faithfulness.

In another context, speaking to the Ephesian elders on the coast of Miletus before his departure for Rome, Paul urges them, "Pay careful attention to yourselves and to all the flock" (Acts 20:28). Similarly, he writes to Timothy, "Keep a close watch on yourself" (1 Tim. 4:16). In other words, scrutinize yourself constantly to ensure that you approach your calling with the utmost seriousness and solemnity.

Why is this calling so serious? Because every aspect of pastoral ministry is performed "in the presence of God and of Christ Jesus, who is to judge the living and the dead, and by his appearing and his kingdom" (2 Tim. 4:1). Paul, in effect, escorts Timothy into an ancient courtroom and says, "The full case of the entirety of your ministry, Timothy, will be drawn up against you in the court of God, where Christ Jesus is the Judge."

This is a summons for every man of God who has been called to the lofty yet humbling task of proclaiming the unsearchable riches of God—to stand in the eternal courtroom of "his presence." The pastor will not have a team of lawyers to argue his case or witnesses to testify of his good works. Still, the whole of his ministry—every sermon preached, every prayer prayed, every deed performed—will be open before the examining, flaming eyes of Christ (Rev. 19:12).

This isn't meant to frighten those contemplating a call to ministry, or seminarians preparing to enter the church, or even those who have been fulfilling their pastoral charge for decades. This charge reminds us of the seriousness with which we must view the calling of the representatives of Christ in the world. Ministry isn't a quick way to make a buck. The church isn't a fast track to renown or notoriety.

God elevates the call to serve the church to a level of eternal scrutiny, warning us to think twice before beginning the journey: "Not many of you should become teachers, my brothers, for you know that we who teach will be judged with greater strictness" (James 3:1). All ministry is to be carried out with constant mindfulness that everything we do is under the watchful eye of God. Therefore, no argument is sustainable for a lackadaisical attitude of wasting time on frivolous things at the expense of tending the flock of God.

"Preach the Word"

Paul distills the pastor's paramount task to a single phrase: "Preach the word" (2 Tim. 4:2). Such a simple statement, yet the pulse of every undershepherd of Christ. A preacher is to herald the word!

The word translated "preach" is the Greek verb meaning "herald, proclaim, and announce publicly." During the Roman Empire, the word *kēryssō* was often associated with those sent from the emperor's imperial court to publicly deliver a message to the people.

Paul writes that he was "appointed a preacher" (1 Tim. 2:7; 2 Tim. 1:11). He didn't choose to be a preacher. He was overwhelmed with a call directly from Christ to "carry [Christ's] name before the Gentiles and kings and the children of Israel" (Acts 9:15). This is the foremost duty of every pastor, to carry the name of Christ to the people by heralding the message of good news.

What is it we herald?

Paul designates the object of our message as "the word" (2 Tim. 4:2). That is, "all Scripture" (2 Tim. 3:16). Paul's sermons were not filled with intellectual platitudes of man's seeming superior wisdom. He wrote, "I, when I came to you, brothers, did not come proclaiming to you the testimony of God with lofty speech or wisdom" (1 Cor. 2:1). Lest anyone think gospel heralds have a message of mere interpretive opinion or suggestion, we're reminded that "what we proclaim is not ourselves, but Jesus Christ as Lord" (2 Cor. 4:5). Nothing should stand as a dam between the refreshing truth of God and the arid lands of the human heart. Only the unceasing proclamation of Christ is sufficient to quench such longing thirst.

It has been said that the Puritans were "spiritual surgeons" because they used the scalpel of God's word to dissect the minds, emotions, wills, and affections of their hearers, applying the healing and cleansing balm of the word of God.[3]

---

3 Ferguson, *Some Pastors and Teachers*, 174.

How often are we to proclaim the word? "In season and out of season" (2 Tim. 4:2).

Pastors are to broadcast every jot and tittle of God's word when the message is *in* and when the message is *out*. When those around you are interested and when they aren't interested. When the message is popular and when it's not popular. The whims of the people must never determine the frequency and substance of preaching. "For the time is coming," says Paul, "when people will not endure sound teaching, but having itching ears they will accumulate for themselves teachers to suit their own passions, and will turn away from listening to the truth and wander off into myths" (2 Tim. 4:3–4). Regardless of the popularity of the message, the pastor is to be ready "in season and out of season" to "reprove, rebuke, and exhort" (2 Tim. 4:2). As with a military guard or a watchman on a tower warning of impending danger to the city, there's no off-season for the pastor. There is only absolute fearlessness.

To "reprove" is to reveal the sinfulness of sin. To "rebuke" is to strike the conscience of the sinner with the veracity of gospel truth. To "exhort" is to encourage the heart and mind that "he who began a good work in you will bring it to completion at the day of Jesus Christ" (Phil. 1:6). Striking a blow against sin, appealing to the conscience, and then encouraging the heart in Christ are all the pastor's job. This job is not always fun. Sometimes it can even be miserable. But regardless of the circumstances, a constant and abiding joy resides within the calling of God upon our lives in the realization that we are making the church beautiful by feeding the flock of God.

Endure

In contrast to those with "itching ears" and those who "will turn away from listening to the truth," Timothy is told, "Always be sober-minded, endure suffering, do the work of an evangelist, fulfill your ministry" (2 Tim. 4:3–5). Paul's penetrating words are just as applicable to us. During the confusion and denial of the truth, we must be clear-minded and stable in our thinking—ready to endure any suffering and rejection that may befall us and dedicating ourselves to faithful gospel proclamation. We must endure. This is specifically applicable not only to all pastors and those in ministry but also to all who desire to live godly lives—endure!

There is a reward for such endurance. "There is laid up for me the crown of righteousness, which the Lord, the righteous judge, will award to me on that day, and not only to me but also to all who have loved his appearing" (2 Tim. 4:8). Our reward is Christ himself—in all his glory, majesty, splendor, loveliness, and beauty. This is why we press on, though it is sometimes difficult, often heartbreaking, and increasingly challenging—we press on for the prize of a crown to cast at the feet of our Lord.

Charles Haddon Spurgeon, lecturing to his students at his Pastor's College, said this:

> If any student in this room could be content to be a newspaper editor or a grocer or a farmer or a doctor or a lawyer or a senator or a king, in the name of heaven and earth let him go his way. He is not the man in whom dwells the Spirit of God in its fullness, for a man so filled with God would utterly weary of any pursuit but that for which his inmost soul pants. If, on the other hand, you can say for all the wealth of both the Indies you could not and dare not espouse any other calling so as to put aside from preaching the gospel of Jesus Christ, then depend on it. If other things be equally satisfactory you have the signs of this apostleship. We must feel that woe is unto us if we preach not the gospel.

He continued,

> The Word of God must be unto us as a fire in our bones, otherwise
> if we undertake the ministry we shall be unhappy in it, shall be
> unable to bear the self-denials incident to it and shall be of little
> service to those among whom we minister. I speak of self-denials
> and well I may, for the true pastor's work is full of them and with-
> out a love to his calling he will soon succumb and either leave the
> drudgery or move on in discontent, burdened with a monotony
> as tiresome as that of a blind horse in a mill.[4]

If you are a pastor, do you love your calling to serve the grand
plan of God within his church? If you aren't a pastor, do you love the
undershepherd God has placed over you to watch over and care for
your soul? Are you committed to listening to and heeding his words
of warning and counsel? Are you committed to taking him before
the throne of grace and praying for his faithfulness and holiness?

Feeding the flock of God is a fundamental duty in contributing
to the beauty and loveliness of the church. As God's truth is proclaimed, men and women are saved and sanctified, and the church
is made beautiful.

4   Charles Haddon Spurgeon, *Lectures to My Students* (London: Passmore and Alabaster, 1875),
    23–24.

10

Good News

*How beautiful upon the mountains
are the feet of him who brings good news.*

ISAIAH 52:7

THE NEW TESTAMENT is unmistakably clear that God has called his church to be the principal agency for heralding the gospel of Christ. When Christ issued his commission to his disciples in Matthew 28:18–20, this command would stand for his church in all subsequent generations. These disciples were the church's nucleus, and upon Christ's ascension to his Father, this little band would serve as his representatives upon earth.

Jesus knew that his followers of the first century would not themselves be able to "make disciples of all nations" (Matt. 28:19). Being "witnesses . . . to the end of the earth" would take more than a millennium to accomplish (Acts 1:8). For that reason, Christ added a long-range promise: "Behold, I am with you always, to the end of the age" (Matt. 28:20).

From Pentecost forward, the book of Acts is replete with accounts of "end of the earth" evangelism. The Spirit-filled apostles were witnesses in Jerusalem, all Judea, Samaria, and beyond (Acts 1:8). While Pentecost is certainly not the beginning of the church, it is her launching into all the earth. What had been primarily a localized church now became a universal church encompassing neighboring nations and beyond.

The believers in the church of Acts were zealous and passionate proclaimers of the good news of Jesus Christ. Peter's enemies told him and the other apostles, "You have filled Jerusalem with your teaching" (Acts 5:28). In response to their evangelistic efforts, Paul and his fellow missionaries were accused of turning the world upside down (Acts 17:6). As a result, "the Lord added to their number day by day those who were being saved" (Acts 2:47).

Whatever happened to the earnest plea to unbelievers to repent and come to Christ that was so stunningly characteristic of the early church? Have we assumed that the church shouldn't take the Lord's commission as seriously as we once did because of our technologically advanced age? After all, the Bible has been translated into countless languages. Missionaries and missionary-sending agencies have thrown a net over the known world, and the advent of mass media has broken down barriers that once existed between people groups and national borders. Is the church still under the commission to be witnesses to the end of the earth?

The Gospel of God

Paul's introduction to his letter to the church in Rome makes it quite apparent that the entire epistle's theme is the good news of "the gospel of God" (Rom. 1:1). Bracketing Romans is the apostle's reminder to his readers that he was called to be "set apart for the gospel of God" (1:1) and a "minister of Christ Jesus . . . in the priestly service of the gospel of God" (15:16). This good news of the gospel is

- "the good news of the kingdom of God" (Luke 16:16),
- "good news . . . of Jesus Christ" (Acts 8:12),
- "good news of peace" (Acts 10:36),
- "the gospel of the grace of God" (Acts 20:24),
- "the gospel of his Son" (Rom. 1:9),
- "the gospel of your salvation" (Eph. 1:13),
- "the gospel of the glory of the blessed God" (1 Tim. 1:11).

Surrounded by *bad* news at every turn, the church has been entrusted with *good* news, the good news of the gospel, which finds its foundation in God himself. The gospel is not an earthly message but a heavenly message. Paul says that this is the "gospel *of God*" (Rom. 1:1). The gospel is *about* God—his holiness, love, grace, wrath, and righteousness. But Paul's main emphasis here is that the gospel is *from* God. He is the single author and architect of the gospel. The gospel doesn't originate in the church. The church doesn't devise the gospel. The church hasn't crafted the gospel. The gospel is a message given to the bride of Christ announcing his mediatorial triumph over sin, death, and the world.

The word translated "gospel" is a compound in Greek, *euangelion*. The prefix *eu* means "good." The primary root word *angelion* means "messenger" or "message." When those two words are placed together, the word *gospel* simply means "good news." The gospel is the good news of salvation through God's Son, Jesus Christ. It is the message that sinners can be rescued from God's wrath against sin through the sacrificial, substitutionary death of Jesus Christ upon the cross and his triumphant resurrection from the dead. This isn't only good news; it's beautifully good news. We will never hear anything more surpassingly beautiful than the truth that Jesus Christ is a willing liberator and Savior of sinners.

What specifically is the message of God's beautiful gospel?

God sent his Son, the second person of the Trinity, the Lord Jesus Christ, to rescue sinners. He was born of a virgin and lived a sinlessly perfect and obedient life under the law. He was crucified on a cross as a substitute to pay the penalty of God's wrath against the sins of all those who would ever believe. In his body, he bore on that tree the punishment due to sinners, and his perfect righteousness was imputed to them, making them acceptable in the sight of God. He was buried in a borrowed tomb and on the third day rose from the dead. He ascended back to the authority and power of the right hand of his Father to intercede for all believers. Now, everyone who by faith "calls on the name of the Lord will be saved" (Rom. 10:13).

No church has the freedom to tamper with, tweak, add to, or subtract from the good news of Jesus Christ—we are just to herald it. For there is nothing more beautiful and lovely in the sight of God than the extricating of sinners from the kingdom of darkness and delivering them to the kingdom of light.

Martin Luther explains the gospel this way:

> *Evangel* (gospel) is a Greek word that means a good message, good tidings, good news, a good report, which one sings and tells with rejoicing. So when David overcame the huge Goliath, the good report and the comforting news came among the Jewish people that their terrible enemy had been slain, that they had been delivered, and that joy and peace had been given to them; and they sang and danced and were happy because of this.

Joy accompanies good news and is the response to the good news. In response to the news that the ark was being brought up to Jerusalem, joy ignited dance within David as he worshiped before the Lord (2 Sam. 6:14). The same response rings through the corridors of heaven when sinners are born again. Jesus said, "I tell you, there is joy before the angels of God over one sinner who repents" (Luke 15:10). Luther comments:

> So the *evangel* (gospel) of God . . . is also a good message and report. The gospel has resounded in all the world, proclaimed by the apostles. It tells of a true David who fought with sin, death, and the devil, overcame them, and thereby delivered, without any merit of their own, all those who were held captive in sin, were plagued by death, and were overpowered by the devil. He made them righteous, gave them life, and saved them.[1]

Luther details the very essence of the gospel—the good news of deliverance from eternal destruction at the hands of a holy God. Such beautiful news causes believing hearts to swell and surge with extolling praise and joy before the Lord.

That is the gospel.

Words Are Necessary

Words are necessary to communicate this good news. Paul asks:

> How then will they call on him in whom they have not believed? And how are they to believe in him of whom they have never heard? And how are they to hear without someone preaching? And how are they to preach unless they are sent? As it is written, "How beautiful are the feet of those who preach the good news." (Rom. 10:14–15)

With surgical precision, after establishing that "everyone who calls on the name of the Lord will be saved" (Rom. 10:13), Paul

---

1 Ewald Plass, *What Luther Says: A Practical In-Home Anthology for the Active Christian* (St. Louis, MO: Concordia, 1959), 561.

presents the logical progression of heralding the good news. Those who "call on the name of the Lord" can "be saved"; only those who have "believed" in him can call upon him; only those who have "heard" of him can "believe in him"; only those who have "a preacher" can rightly "hear" of him. Finally, no preacher can "preach" the saving good news of the gospel who has not been "sent" by God. More concisely, Paul is saying that if God did not send preachers, no one would hear; if no one heard, no one would believe; if no one believed, no one would call upon the name of the Lord; and if no one called upon the name of the Lord, no one would be saved.

Within this logic emerges the calling of the church.

Drawing from Isaiah 52:7, "How beautiful upon the mountains / are the feet of him who brings good news," Paul highlights not the beauty of a preacher's feet per se but the wondrous beauty of the good news that those feet carry to the nations. Isaiah was reflecting on Israel's glorious deliverance from years of captivity and bondage—this was good news. For Paul, salvation from sin is the good news he was called to herald and which he entrusted to the church as well to proclaim.

The impetus for our gospel zeal is the promise that

all the ends of the earth shall see
    the salvation of our God. (Isa. 52:10)

All evangelistic and missionary endeavors are fueled by the confidence that Christ is enthroned as the head of the church and has promised to ransom men and women from "every tribe and language and people and nation" (Rev. 5:8–9). This assurance fueled John Calvin to write to the king when evangelistic efforts were harshly suppressed in his homeland of France:

Indeed, we are quite aware of what . . . lowly little men we are.
. . . But our doctrine must tower unvanquished above all the glory
and above all the might of the world, for it is not of us, but of
the living God and his Christ whom the Father has appointed to
"rule from sea to sea, and from the rivers even to the ends of the
earth" (Ps. 72:8).[2]

"It is not of us," Calvin wrote. There's such a God-centeredness to
the gospel that we cannot claim it as our own. It didn't originate
with the church, for we merely "have this treasure in jars of clay,
to show that the surpassing power belongs to God and not to us"
(2 Cor. 4:7). The gospel is God's gospel.

Peter stood before the Sanhedrin and boldly declared, "There is no
other name under heaven given among men by which we must be
saved" (Acts 4:12). Paul likewise maintained that "there is one God,
and there is one mediator between God and men, the man Christ
Jesus" (1 Tim. 2:5). The gospel proclaimed by the church is exclusive
and embraces all of life. The gospel of Christ is the only gospel that
will reconcile us to God and bring us peace and salvation.

A Lost World

The great Puritan commentator Matthew Henry devised a prayer
method that offers prayers for "the lost world," specifically for the
advance of the gospel to foreign nations and the growth of the church
worldwide through salvation. With a scriptural framework, Henry
purposefully structured his prayers so that those praying would be
reciting the words of Scripture. Listen to his prayers for the lost world:

2 John Calvin, prefatory address to King Francis, in *Institutes of the Christian Religion*, ed. John T.
McNeill, trans. Ford Lewis Battles (Philadelphia: Westminster Press, 1960), 13.

Let the people praise thee, O God, yea, let all the people praise thee.

O let thy salvation and thy righteousness be openly showed in the sight of the heathen, and let all the ends of the earth see the salvation of our God.

O give thy Son the heathen for his inheritance, and the uttermost parts of the earth for his possession; for thou hast said, it is a light thing for him to raise up the tribes of Jacob, and to restore the preserved of Israel, but thou wilt give him for a light to the Gentiles.

Let all the kingdoms of this world become the kingdoms of the Lord, and of his Christ.

O let the gospel be preached unto every creature; for how shall men believe in him of whom they have not heard? And how shall they hear without preachers? And how shall they preach except they be sent? And who shall send forth labourers, but the Lord of the harvest?

O let the earth be full of the knowledge of the Lord, as the waters cover the sea.[3]

These selections are but a small collection of the numerous prayers that could be lifted from the Psalms—prayers that speak of God's sovereign dominion over the earth and the anointed King's future reign over the nations. Quintessentially Puritan, these prayers reveal the heart that seventeenth- and eighteenth-century believers had for the advance of the good news of Jesus Christ to the ends of the earth. The Puritans fervently believed prayer was the primary way

3   Matthew Henry, *A Method for Prayer*, in *The Complete Works of the Rev. Matthew Henry*, vol. 2 (1855; repr., Grand Rapids, MI: Baker, 1979), 48–49.

the church could be involved in global evangelization. William Gurnall said:

> Let thy prayers walk over the vast ocean. . . . Visit the churches of Christ abroad . . . where Adam's sin threw them with us, without any attempt made as yet upon them by the gospel for their recovery, and carry their deplored condition before the Lord. Our Drake is famous for compassing the earth with his ship in a few years; thou mayest by thy prayers every day, and make a more gainful voyage of it too than he did.[4]

By entrusting his church with the task of heralding the gospel, God has chosen her to be an honored vessel to house and disseminate his treasure (2 Cor. 4:7).

To those who are hungry, the bride says, "Come." To those who are thirsty, the bride says, "Come." To those who desire to drink of the water of life, the bride says, "Come" (Rev. 22:17).

R. B. Kuiper sums up the matter well:

> All that the church does, and can do, when it brings the gospel to lost men is to plant and to water. For results, it is completely dependent on God, who alone can give the increase. But even thus the church is God's co-laborer. Under God, to be sure, yet also together with God, it labors for the highest of all ends, the glory of the Most High.[5]

---

4 William Gurnall, *The Christian in Complete Armour*, vol. 2 (1658; repr., Edinburgh: Banner of Truth, 2002), 524–25. Francis Drake (1540–1596) was an English sea captain who circled the earth from 1577 to 1580. See also Joel R. Beeke and Mark Jones, "Puritan Prayers for World Missions," chap. 47 in *A Puritan Theology* (Grand Rapids, MI: Reformation Heritage, 2012), 769.

5 R. B. Kuiper, *The Glorious Body of Christ* (London: Banner of Truth, 1966), 243.

11

In Remembrance

Do this in remembrance of me.

1 CORINTHIANS 11:24

THERE ARE COUNTLESS WAYS in which God enriches, beautifies, and sanctifies his church. We have already discovered how the ministries of the Father, Son, and Holy Spirit; the gift of faithful leaders; the proclamation of the word; and the heartfelt worship of the saints all combine to present the bride of Christ without wrinkle or blemish. God also uses additional means that we sometimes shove to the periphery of church life or take for granted. Those means include the two ordinances of the church—baptism and the Lord's Supper.

The ordinances of baptism and the Lord's Supper are two specific ways in which God accomplishes his beautifying work within his church. Some traditions call these two mandates sacraments to denote that they are *holy* things and should therefore be kept holy by the church. Regardless of what they are labeled, these two ordinances are taught in Scripture and are reserved by God to be practiced exclusively by the church.

In his seminal work *The Glorious Body of Christ*, R. B. Kuiper wrote: "Let it be understood that the sacraments add nothing to the Word of God. There is nothing contained in the sacraments which is not contained in the Word. When the church administers the sacraments, it proclaims visibly the very same gospel which it proclaims audibly in its preaching."[1] In other words, the ordinances are visible manifestations that God, in Christ, desires to commune with his people by imaging forth his gospel through these means of grace.

Baptism

Baptism has been quite a controversial subject throughout church history, as many traditions have adopted varied ways of observing this ordinance. The basis for baptism comes as a commission and command from Christ before his ascension:

> All authority in heaven and on earth has been given to me. Go therefore and make disciples of all nations, *baptizing* them in the name of the Father and of the Son and of the Holy Spirit, teaching them to observe all that I have commanded you. And behold, I am with you always, to the end of the age. (Matt. 28:18–20)

The followers of Christ are endowed with a divine responsibility to disciple new believers by teaching them that baptism is their first act of obedience in this new life of faith. Baptism is not a suggested practice but a clear command, for discipleship is not complete without baptism.

True disciples have been saved by grace through faith, and baptism is the external testimony and public witness of that inward saving faith wrought within the heart by the Holy Spirit.

---

1   R. B. Kuiper, *The Glorious Body of Christ* (London: Banner of Truth, 1966), 202–3.

The Greek word for baptism is *baptizō* and refers to the immersion or submersion of fabric into dye to change its appearance. The term has also been associated with bathing or washing with water. Interestingly, it appears around 200 BC in a Greek physician's text in a sort of ancient recipe for pickles. The author of the formula instructs readers that the vegetable should be "dipped" (*baptō*) to wash it and then "baptized" (*baptizō*), or submerged permanently into a vinegar solution, for the pickling process to occur, resulting in a permanent change to the vegetable. Both Greek verbs signal a change. While the first is a temporary change, the latter is permanent. When used in the New Testament, *baptizō* often refers to our union and identification with Christ rather than water baptism. A lasting change occurs as a new follower of Christ is brought into union with him and immersed into his death and resurrection (Rom. 6:3–4).

Baptism is beautifully associated with repentance and faith. In Matthew 3, multitudes come to John the Baptist to be baptized as a symbol of their repentance from sin and turning to God (Matt. 3:6). Baptism is a symbol that points to saving faith; it is not the conveyer of saving grace. This becomes clear when Paul states: "By grace you have been saved through faith. And this is not of your own doing; it is the gift of God, not a result of *works*, so that no one may boast" (Eph. 2:8–9). If salvation were contingent upon baptism, then salvation would be contingent upon our works and not God's grace. In response to the Philippian jailer's question "Sirs, what must I do to be saved?" Paul and Silas responded, "Believe in the Lord Jesus, and you will be saved" (Acts. 16:30–31). Therefore, baptism comes after and points back to salvation, repentance, and faith. It was said of "those who received [Peter's] word" that they were then "baptized" (Acts 2:41), and of those who "believed Philip as he preached good news about the kingdom of God and the name of Jesus Christ" that they were then "baptized, both men and women" (Acts 8:12). Biblical baptism signifies a turning away from sin, a full-fledged embrace of Christ, and a believer's willingness to identify with him in his death, burial, and resurrection so that we can now "walk in newness of life" (Rom. 6:4).

For John Calvin, baptism was primarily a seal of the divine promise of salvation and, therefore, part of God's mysterious purposes. By the Puritan age, baptism was often practiced privately. In their continued reform of church worship, the Puritans brought baptism out of the shadows and into the light of public, corporate worship. The Puritans labored to draw a clear distinction between outward baptism and the inward reality of faith. While the baptismal waters are a symbol, genuine faith brings that symbol to life as we identify with Christ in his death, burial, and resurrection. Without faith, the symbol is lost and we instead become accountable before God for the act of a false profession. Therefore, while water baptism points to the beauty of the gospel, it does not save.

In obedience to his Father, Jesus himself submitted to baptism, not in identification with his own repentance, for no repentance was necessary from the sinless Son of God, but in identification with those he came to rescue. Jesus sets the example for us. Therefore, you cannot willfully neglect obedience to baptism and claim consistently to be a follower of Christ. "Everyone who acknowledges me before men, I also will acknowledge before my Father who is in heaven, but whoever denies me before men, I also will deny before my Father who is in heaven" (Matt. 10:32–33). There's an inherent beauty in our obedience to the words of Christ and our acknowledgment of him as our Savior and Lord.

The final glimpse we have of the Ethiopian eunuch after he was baptized shows that he "went on his way rejoicing" (Acts 8:39). Obedience to the commands of Christ brings abiding joy and pleasure within the obedient. If you recall your baptism, perhaps you felt similar joy welling up inside your heart as you emerged from the waters. The perfection of the beauty of the gospel has manifested itself within your very heart, and baptism was a public witness to that eternal transformation.

What could be more beautiful?

While odd and perhaps even off-putting to the world, entering the baptismal waters in the confession of our faith and identification with the death, burial, and resurrection of our Lord is a means by which we behold the magnificent beauty of Christ and mirror that beauty outwardly in public testimony.

Baptism demonstrates that you love Christ and are willing to obey him. In some cultures, baptism is a mark of death upon believers as it is the official sign that you are a follower and disciple of Christ. This obedient act says, "I am willing to follow you, Lord, even to death if necessary."

Baptism beautifies the church in several ways. First, it exalts Christ by being a visible expression and reminder of his death, burial, and resurrection. Second, it energizes onlookers to obey Christ by making their own public confession of faith. Third, baptism announces the gospel. Apart from the gospel's proclamation in preaching, baptism is the most visual portrayal of the gospel possessed by the church. Fourth, baptism serves as a sign and a warning—a sign that forgiveness is available to all who place their faith in Christ, and a warning that unless you repent, "you will all likewise perish" (Luke 13:3).

As God's gift to his church, baptism is how he incorporates us into his fold, strengthens his body, beautifies his church, and draws more to himself.

The Lord's Supper

A second ordinance of the church is the Lord's Supper (1 Cor. 11:20). In the book of Acts, this supper is identified by the phrase, "the breaking of bread" (2:42, 46; 20:7, 11). In 1 Corinthians 10:16, it's also referred to as "communion," from the Greek word that means "fellowship" or "communion." Finally, it is sometimes called "the table of the Lord" (1 Cor. 10:21) and the Eucharist, from the Greek word for "give thanks" (Mark 14:23).

The apostle Paul offers a full explanation of the Lord's Supper in 1 Corinthians 11:

> For I received from the Lord what I also delivered to you, that the Lord Jesus on the night when he was betrayed took bread, and when he had given thanks, he broke it, and said, "This is my body, which is for you. Do this in remembrance of me." In the same way also he took the cup, after supper, saying, "This cup is the new covenant in my blood. Do this, as often as you drink it, in remembrance of me." For as often as you eat this bread and drink the cup, you proclaim the Lord's death until he comes. (vv. 23–26)

Paul recalls the meal the Lord Jesus celebrated with his disciples the night before his death (Luke 22:14–23). Originally the meal of Passover, this old covenant feast was transformed by Jesus into a meal of infinitely greater significance. Whereas the Passover meal was celebrated with loved ones as a time to remember, reflect on, and recite the account of Israel's deliverance from Egyptian bondage (Ex. 12:1–4), the Lord's Supper remembers the cross of Christ as the place of deliverance from sin, death, and hell. The Passover was about temporal deliverance; the Lord's Supper points to eternal deliverance. The Passover lambs had to be slaughtered every year;

the Lord's Supper points to Christ, who died a sufficient death for all time.

The Lord's Supper radiates with the glory of Christ—in flesh and blood—causing believers to reflect back to when their sins were atoned for by God's spotless Lamb while also looking forward to the great marriage supper of the Lamb, when we shall bask together in the resplendent glory of our Father.

The simple elements of bread and the cup become a beautifying influence on the church as the supper demonstrates our remembering, loving, and examining.

Remembering

Biblical scholars believe the first epistle to the Corinthians was written before Matthew, Mark, and Luke—the Synoptic Gospels—and thereby may serve as the church's first instructions regarding the Lord's Supper. Paul cites Jesus's words "Do this, as often as you drink it, in *remembrance* of me" (1 Cor. 11:25). The supper becomes a path to congregational beauty as we come together to remember Christ.

Now, you might say, "How could I ever forget Christ?" But the reality is that it is all too easy in the ordinary course of our lives to forget those we hold most dear. Through the centuries, artists in every culture have depicted Jesus through various mediums, trying to construct his likeness. We need look no further than to the Lord's Supper to see Jesus, for through this celebratory meal, he has left us a portrait of himself—to remember him. The very elements point to Christ. Without diving into the varied views, we may say that the bread represents his incarnate sinless flesh nailed to the cross, and the cup signifies the blood that poured forth for the atonement of sin. When eaten and drunk amid corporate worship, these elements together become one of the most explicit pictures of Jesus that the church retains.

Not only do we remember his sacrificial death, but we also remember (or revisit) the very place of our forgiveness. Reflecting on the frequency of the old covenant sacrificial system, the writer of Hebrews states, "Every priest stands daily at his service, offering *repeatedly* the same sacrifices, which can never take away sins" (Heb. 10:11). The countless goats, bulls, and lambs offered in sacrifice to God in the old covenant had to be presented repeatedly because they never fully atoned for sin. However, Jesus said: "This cup is the *new covenant* in my blood. Do this, as often as you drink it, in remembrance of me" (1 Cor. 11:25). The "new covenant" is the eternal promise,

For I will be merciful toward their iniquities,
    and I will remember their sins no more. (Heb. 8:12)

The supper is the facilitator of our remembrance. And while we remember, the Lord forgets—our sin. The bread and cup are our reminders that sinners are forgiven, never to be unforgiven, completely righteous, never to be unrighteous. How could anything be more lovely than that gospel-soaked truth?

Paul adds, "For as often as you eat this bread and drink the cup, you proclaim the Lord's death until he comes" (1 Cor. 11:26). The Lord's Supper causes us to remember the words of the angels to the disciples at the ascension of Jesus into the glory of his Father, "This Jesus, who was taken up from you into heaven, will come in the same way as you saw him go into heaven" (Acts 1:11). The supper drives our hearts to remember the day when

the Lord himself will descend from heaven with a cry of command,
    with the voice of an archangel, and with the sound of the trumpet

of God. And the dead in Christ will rise first. Then we who are alive, who are left, will be caught up together with them in the clouds to meet the Lord in the air, and so we will always be with the Lord. (1 Thess. 4:16–17)

Remembering the truth that Jesus is returning to receive his own and judge the world motivates the church to "proclaim the Lord's death." That is, through the supper—calling to mind his death, burial, and resurrection—we herald the gospel until we meet the Lord in the air.

If "the breaking of bread" throughout the book of Acts refers to believers celebrating the Lord's Supper, then they began by celebrating it every day. Later, in Acts 20:7, the early church "on the first day of the week . . . gathered together to break bread." Scripture nowhere specifies the frequency with which a local congregation should come together to partake of the bread and the cup. Some churches observe it every Sunday, while others may observe it only twice or three times per year. It's often argued that if a church celebrates the supper too often, it may merely become an empty ritual. But it's possible for anything we do in the Christian life to become an empty ritual. Things like Bible reading, prayer, or worship can become mindless activities we check off of our spiritual to-do lists. But there is a beauty in communing with the Lord around his table, eating the bread, drinking from the cup, celebrating deliverance from sin through Christ at the cross, remembering his eternally sufficient sacrifice to conquer death, anticipating his future kingdom. These are all things the church should enjoy together often as she seeks to be transformed into the image of Christ "from one degree of glory to another" (2 Cor. 3:18).

Hence, when you come to the Lord's Table and by faith remember his suffering and death, remember his newly established covenant for the eternal forgiveness of sin, and remember that he is returning soon, bear in mind the stunning words of 1 Peter 2:24: "He himself bore our sins in his body on the tree, that we might die to sin and live to righteousness. By his wounds you have been healed."

Loving

Before offering instructions on the Lord's Supper, Paul addresses significant divisional issues within the church of Corinth. While meals such as this were meant to foster the sweetness of fellowship that comes when God's people meet with him in worship, some in Corinth used it as a time to engage in drunkenness and to demonstrate partiality among the people (1 Cor. 11:18, 21). Factions were making the Corinthians rife with sin and divided the body of Christ.

Paul reminds them, "Because there is one bread, we who are many are *one* body, for we all partake of the *one* bread" (1 Cor. 10:17). The early church passed around one common loaf, and members would pinch a small piece off to celebrate the supper. Through this visible representation, Paul reminds them that they are *one* body, and their fractured state is a blemish on the purity of the church and a stain upon what the supper means. Because of the division within the congregation and their selfish gluttony (1 Cor. 11:18–22), the evident result is that "when you come together, it is not the Lord's Supper that you eat" (v. 20). In other words, their division and excess at the supper contradicts the mutual love portrayed in the supper itself. Paul addresses the Corinthians negatively, pointing out their sin and division. Stated positively, the Lord's Supper should be a demonstration of believers' love for one another.

The very symbols present within the meal highlight the selfless, sacrificial love poured forth by Christ on the cross. Are you coming to the table divided, fractured, and in opposition to one another?

The Lord's Table is one of the foremost places within the church to gather in mutual love and reconciliation. This is why the Lord's Supper is not to be celebrated alone, for it is a congregational meal to demonstrate and foster genuine love among the people of God. In our Lord's Sermon on the Mount, he taught: "If you are offering your gift at the altar and there remember that your brother has something against you, leave your gift there before the altar and go. First be reconciled to your brother, and then come and offer your gift" (Matt. 5:23–24). At the table, ask forgiveness of the spouse you fought with before worship began, or the brother you disagreed with politically, or the sister you talked about in an ungodly way. At the table, we're reminded that the church is one, and our mutual love radiates forth to display a beautiful bride before a watching world.

Examining

For this type of mutual love and reconciliation to be present, each of us must examine himself or herself. Paul offers a warning, "Whoever, therefore, eats the bread or drinks the cup of the Lord in an unworthy manner will be guilty concerning the body and blood of the Lord" (1 Cor. 11:27–28). It's possible to come to the table like the hypocritical Corinthians, unloving, unforgiving, and for selfish indulgence and show. Therefore, Paul implores, "Let a person examine himself, then, and so eat of the bread and drink of the cup. For anyone who eats and drinks without discerning the body eats and drinks judgment on himself" (1 Cor. 11:28–29).

By examining ourselves, we perform a mental and internal survey of our relationship with Christ, our relationships with others, and our private and public sins. Now, the Lord's Supper isn't for the sinless—for no one is without sin—but is for those who have thoroughly examined every aspect of their lives, so far as is possible, and confessed and repented of sin with a wholehearted desire to walk with Christ.

Before his arrest, as Jesus was celebrating this meal with his disciples, they began to argue among themselves over who was the greatest in the kingdom (Luke 22:24). As the disciples were flaunting their supposed spiritual superiority, Jesus warned Peter that he would deny him three times, that they all would scatter, and that none of them would stick with him all the way to death. Just a few hours later, they all fell asleep in the garden when Jesus instructed them to pray that "you may not enter temptation" (Luke 22:40). We sometimes read accounts like this, scratching our heads and saying to ourselves, "I would never do that." However, on closer examination, we quickly discover that we too are spiritually weak and vulnerable to sin, like the disciples. These examples remind us that there are no sinless men or women within the church, nor are only innocent people permitted to partake of the bread and cup. But those who are allowed are those who struggle endlessly with the plague of sin and have properly examined themselves, have confessed what they know, and desire to walk the path of repentance.

While baptism identifies us with the death, burial, and resurrection of our Lord and the testimony of faith wrought within our hearts, the Lord's Supper is the frequent reminder that believers must remember the Lord, love one another, and continually deal with their sin. In these ways, both baptism and the Lord's Supper are visible ordinances whereby the Holy Spirit sanctifies believers. Through our participation in both, the Lord has provided a way in which his bride is inseparably linked to his cross and resurrection as the ultimate glory of her beauty.

12

Walking Worthy

Walk in a manner worthy of the calling
to which you have been called.

EPHESIANS 4:1

OVER THE LAST HALF CENTURY, the world of evangelicalism has witnessed a burst of progress. Several decades after World War II, modern Protestant denominations experienced a theologically conservative rebirth out of the liberalism of their forebears. Vibrant interest in biblical doctrine, return to expositional preaching, focus on the local church, emphasis upon missions and evangelism, and engagement in the public square have all been the fruit of this resurgence. These seemingly fruitful years have witnessed unparalleled growth in theological institutions, an explosion of Christian publishing, an unending evangelical conference circuit, the emergence of countless para-church ministries, and a mounting effort to engage in political affairs.

While many of these trends have been greatly helpful in facilitating church ministries, encouraging pastors, and training believers, is the church actually *better*? That is, are we more holy? Do we love the church more deeply? Do we preach better sermons? Do we have a higher view of God? Are we sharing the gospel with our neighbors? In short, is the church as healthy as it seems from the outside?

Many would affirm *yes!* And perhaps that *yes* is fully warranted. However, though outwardly successful in her endeavors, the church is in danger of forsaking a vital element that, if neglected, could lead to untold failures. What is this critical element in this crucial hour?

Walking worthy.

A Heavenly Position

Paul spends the first three chapters of his letter to the Ephesian church assembling a doctrinal framework upon which he will hang principles of right behavior. Paul never offers the *how* without first giving us the *why*. As already discussed, in Ephesians 1, Paul opens the portals of eternity past that we may peer into the plan of the triune God who sovereignly saved those who will make up his church by placing them in Christ. Every line of this chapter is full of rich theological and defining truth for the church.

Continuing a theological doxology begun in chapter 1, Ephesians 2 opens with the acknowledgment: "You were dead in the trespasses and sins" (v. 1) and had no inherent power or ability to reverse your miserable condition apart from the free grace of God, who "made us alive together with Christ" (v. 5). Having been rescued from our depraved state by the gospel of Christ, believers are identified in several ways:

- "fellow citizens" (v. 19)
- "saints" (v. 19)
- "members of the household of God" (v. 19)
- "a holy temple in the Lord" (v. 21)
- "a dwelling place for God by the Spirit" (v. 22)

This exalted position is distinctive, unlike anything we see in the world, and is available only by grace through faith in Christ. Once again, as though to shrink the church back down to size by telling them that they are mere spectators and recipients of this lavished grace, Paul reminds his readers that though the church is a glorious dwelling, Christ alone is the "cornerstone" (v. 20).

This gospel mystery is mind-boggling to Paul. Once hell-bound sinners, the elect are now fellow heirs and "members of the same body, and partakers of the promise in Christ Jesus through the gospel" (Eph. 3:6).

Paul dedicated his whole life and calling to this gospel. The purpose of his calling was that "through the church the manifold wisdom of God might now be made known to the rulers and authorities in the heavenly places" (Eph. 3:10). All the dark forces ("rulers and authorities") of this world that led into transgression and sin now behold this lovely bride ("the church") who has been brought forth in the image of Christ. Now, this militant bride, armed with the "manifold wisdom of God," confronts these dark forces with the glorious good news of the gospel (Eph. 3:10).

These first three chapters of Ephesians are the *why*.

Walking Faithful

What are believers, the church, supposed to do with this good news, this new identity, this power at work within us? *How* are we supposed to live?

With the most emphatic terms possible, having built a solid theological foundation, Paul then writes, "I therefore, a prisoner for the Lord, urge you to walk in a manner worthy of the calling to which you have been called" (Eph. 4:1).

Having described these manifold blessings of God and the Ephesians' knowledge of their identity in Christ, Paul shifts his discussion to how believers are to live. "I therefore," is an intentional turn from the theological to the practical—*how* God's people should live as a result of *who* they are. This whole applicatory section of Ephesians 4:1–6:20 is built upon the firm bedrock of Christ as the cornerstone of his church and the Spirit who empowers such living (Eph. 3:16).

Before urging faithful living, Paul reminds his readers that he is "a prisoner for the Lord" (Eph. 4:1; cf. 3:1) and is enduring "suffering for you, which is your glory" (Eph. 3:13). Paul is not asking for sympathy or even rescue from his circumstances. He's merely saying that there's a cost to living a faithful Christian life. He is not asking his congregation to trod a path he himself has not traveled. He is not a prisoner of Rome but a "prisoner for the Lord." Regardless of the consequences of walking faithfully, our confidence is in our Lord's faithfulness to us, and our commitment is alone to him.

"I . . . urge you to walk." The metaphor of *walking* appears throughout Paul's letters and is always connected with an urgency in the Christian life. Paul understands this urgency. The following admonitions are dispensed not as suggestions or good ideas but as unequivocal commands for faithfulness in *being* and *living as* the body of Christ. This is your obedience in the gospel—you who once *walked* in transgressions and sins (Eph. 2:1–2)—you now must *walk* in the good works God has intended for you (Eph. 2:10).

Throughout the New Testament, the verb "walk" is a present tense Greek word referring to a continuous mode of conduct. The infinitive "to walk" can be rendered "to live." In his instructions to the church, Paul uses "walk" in this way to guarantee that they comprehend what correct Christian living is and what it is not.

A quick survey of Paul's corpus reveals the action of *walking* as a metaphor he often employs to explain the Christian life:

- "Walk properly as in the daytime" (Rom. 13:13).
- "Walk by faith, not by sight" (2 Cor. 5:7).
- "Walk by the Spirit, and you will not gratify the desires of the flesh" (Gal. 5:16).
- "Walk in love" (Eph. 5:2).
- "Walk as children of the light" (Eph. 5:8).
- "Walk in a manner worthy of the Lord" (Col. 1:10).
- "Walk in him" (Col. 2:6).
- "Walk properly before outsiders" (1 Thess. 4:12).

For Paul, "walking" is shorthand for practical Christian living—living out what has been planted within.

Other New Testament writers also employ the same image of walking to define the life of a believer. For instance, John says Christians are not to "walk in darkness" (1 John 1:6; 2:11). Believers should not continue to live in the sin from which they were rescued. In his Gospel record, John teaches that Jesus was the true light for a sin-darkened world (John 1:4–5), and no one can rightly claim to be a true believer and follower of Christ who continues to walk in the sinful darkness.

In contrast, the bride of Christ is to "walk in the light" (1 John 1:7). Those who walk in the light do so because the Spirit of God has regenerated them and given them new life in Christ. When church members' feet are firmly fixed on the path of light, their lives will reflect the glory and majesty of the one who is the light. Your daily actions, attitudes, conversations, thoughts, and works will reflect a light-filled Christlikeness. Walking in the light results in a godly attitude so that, instead of lashing out at difficult people or becoming angry with those who disagree, you're actually brought into "fellowship with one another" (1 John 1:7). All true Christians live and walk in the light.

The Puritans saw themselves as pilgrims in this world, walking with one eye upon the heavenly world to which they were traveling and one eye upon imaging forth Christ to a sinful world. J. I. Packer called this a "pilgrim mentality."[1] He wrote, "Puritans saw themselves as God's pilgrims traveling home, God's warriors battling against the world, the flesh, and the devil; and God's servants under orders to do all the good they could as they went along."[2] While believing they must be salt and light to the world, the Puritans also distanced themselves from this world, viewing themselves as aliens and strangers to a realm so opposed to Christ.

This theme of pilgrimage as being synonymous with the Christian life originates in Scripture (see Gen. 12; Jer. 22; Heb. 11; 1 Pet. 1–2). Most notably, perhaps, it refers to the mentality of the great heroes of faith in Hebrews 11. "These all died in faith, not having received the things promised, but having seen them and greeted them from afar, and having acknowledged that they were strangers and exiles on the earth" (Heb. 11:13).

John Calvin often returned to this pilgrim analogy in his writings. "If heaven is our homeland, what else is the earth but our place of exile?" Calvin asks.[3] Elsewhere, he observes that Paul "teaches us to travel as pilgrims in this world that our celestial heritage may not perish or pass away."[4] Being an exile himself, Calvin well understood the gut-wrenching grief that accompanies living away from one's home-

---

1 Joel R. Beeke and Mark Jones, *A Puritan Theology* (Grand Rapids, MI: Reformation Heritage, 2012), 843.

2 J. I. Packer, "A Man for All Ministries: Richard Baxter, 1615–1691," *Reformation & Revival* 1, no. 1 (1992): 55.

3 John Calvin, *Institutes of the Christian Religion*, ed. John T. McNeill, trans. Ford Lewis Battles (Philadelphia: Westminster Press, 1960), 3.9.4.

4 Calvin, *Institutes*, 3.7.3.

land. Applying that to the Christian life, Calvin believed that any follower of Christ would invariably feel like a stranger in this world as his or her walk will be viewed with suspicion, misunderstanding, and even rejection. Calvin cited Abraham's journey from his native land as a shining example full of instruction and encouragement for those who joined him in earthly pilgrimage. Writing in 1548 to a French nobleman who was considering making the trek from his home to Geneva because of persecution, Calvin said:

> We have an example in our father Abraham. After God had commanded him to abandon his country, his kindred, and everything else, [God] gave him no indication of any reward, but left that for another time. "Go," he said, "to the land I will show you." If it pleases [God] to do the same to us today so that we too must leave our homeland and resettle in an unknown country without knowing what is awaiting us, let us place ourselves in his hands and have him direct our steps. Grant him the honor of trusting him that he will guide us to a safe harbor. Yet you should realize that you will not be coming to a paradise on earth.[5]

Until we reach our eternal home, God has called all of his people to live out the walk of a pilgrim, Calvin believed. A life of consecration, holiness, worship, and obedience to Christ—that is a worthy walk.

By the Spirit

As a result of walking in the light, the body of Christ also walks by the Spirit. At the precise moment of someone's salvation, the Holy Spirit begins to live within that person. Puritan Richard Sibbes believed

---

5 Calvin to a French *Seigneur*, October 18, 1548, in *Selected Works of John Calvin*, ed. H. Beveridge, vol. 5 (repr., Grand Rapids, MI: Baker Academic, 1983), 180.

that at the exact instant the Spirit takes up residence within us, he begins to knit our hearts to God and Jesus Christ. Sibbes explained:

> He [the Spirit] sanctifieth and purifieth, and doth all from the Father and the Son, and knits us to the Father and the Son; to the Son first, and then to the Father . . . because all the communion we have with God is by the Holy Ghost. All the communion that Christ as man had with God was by the Holy Ghost; and all the communion that God hath with us, and we with God is by the Holy Ghost. For the Spirit is the bond of union between Christ and us, and between God and us.[6]

The role of the Spirit is to intimately acquaint us with the Father and the Son. He establishes communion between us and empowers us to walk. When the Spirit is present, he transforms our lives from one degree of glory to another. As he molds us into the image of Christ, the Spirit collectively empowers the church to walk in a Christlike manner.

In Galatians 5:16–26 Paul admonishes us to keep in step with the Spirit:

> But I say, walk by the Spirit, and you will not gratify the desires of the flesh. For the desires of the flesh are against the Spirit, and the desires of the Spirit are against the flesh, for these are opposed to each other, to keep you from doing the things you want to do. But if you are led by the Spirit, you are not under the law. Now the works of the flesh are evident: sexual immorality, impurity, sensuality, idolatry, sorcery, enmity, strife, jealously, fits of anger,

---

6   Richard Sibbes, "A Description of Christ," in *The Complete Works of Richard Sibbes*, ed. Alexander B. Grosart, 7 vols. (1862–1864; repr., Edinburgh: Banner of Truth, 1978–1983), 1:17.

rivalries, dissensions, divisions, envy, drunkenness, orgies, and things like these. I warn you, as I warned you before, that those who do such things will not inherit the kingdom of God. But the fruit of the Spirit is love, joy, peace, patience, kindness, goodness, faithfulness, gentleness, self-control; against such things there is no law. And those who belong to Christ Jesus have crucified the flesh with its passions and desires.

If we live by the Spirit, let us also keep in step with the Spirit. Let us not become conceited, provoking one another, envying one another.

What kind of church would we be if we meditated on and followed Paul's instructions in this key text?

The word "walk" used here is in the present tense in the Greek, indicating that Paul is not speaking of a one-time transaction, like justification, but is pointing to the continual and habitual way of sanctification. Lest we think this is a mere suggestion, Paul uses the imperative mood to indicate that this is a command. Walking suggests progress from one point to another. It's how we transition from our homes to our neighbors' homes or from our living rooms to our kitchens. Living the Christian life within the framework of the church is no different. A believer within the body of Christ who submits to the Spirit's control moves forward in spiritual abundance contributing to the goal of spotlessness within the church. Step-by-step, the Spirit moves us closer and closer to God as he fashions from clay a vessel like the image of Christ.

While it is the Spirit who unleashes the dynamic power to walk in the Christian life, it is the individual Christian who must put one foot in front of the other. The Spirit fills every true believer within the household of faith, but those individual believers must work, teach, pray, and worship, propelling the church into a closer walk and joy in Jesus. The Spirit doesn't work for us, preach for us, evangelize for us, or even worship for us. He empowers his people to do all these things, but it is their responsibility to walk.

To "walk by the Spirit" is to "not gratify the desires of the flesh" (Gal. 5:16). Paul issues the same injunction to the Romans: "Put on the Lord Jesus Christ, and make no provision for the flesh, to gratify its desires" (Rom. 13:14). The apostle sets a contrast in Galatians 6 between those who walk by the flesh and those who "walk by the Spirit." These two walks, or behaviors, are mutually exclusive, so that the whole Christian life is a call to the one way of walking and not the other.

A life characterized by Spirit-led walking is continuously concerned with growing in Christlikeness, having our minds saturated with the truth of God's word, having our hearts enraptured in perpetual doxological praise, giving our lives in service to love and help our neighbors, and glorifying the Lord in all things. To walk in the Spirit is to manifest a life patterned after our perfect example, the Lord Jesus Christ. It is a life whose constant desire is to "be found in him, not having a righteousness of my own that comes from the law, but that which comes through faith in Christ, the righteousness from God that depends on faith" (Phil. 3:9). It is a life whose overarching desire is to "know him and the power of his resurrection . . . becoming like him in his death, that by any means possible I may attain the resurrection from the dead" (Phil. 3:10–11).

If it were not for the command to "walk by the Spirit," every other command of Scripture would be impossible to achieve. Sadly, however, the need for this heavenly empowerment doesn't stop Christians from coasting through life while expecting to receive the blessings of being part of the bride without doing any of the walking.

This worthy walk is a vital element that is missed, misunderstood, and misused in the body of Christ. We often don't take it seriously enough. A church that is beautiful in the eyes of her bridegroom is a church that is walking "in a manner worthy of the calling to which you have been called" (Eph. 4:1). It is living lives that regularly confess sin and preeminently desire to walk according to the Spirit and not according to the flesh. Living lives that reflect their Master and image him forth to a watching world. Living lives that yearn to know him and have his gospel power flow in them for his good pleasure. Living lives that mutually display to all who see that the church is genuinely walking worthy.

13

Blessed Persecution

All who desire to live a godly life in
Christ Jesus will be persecuted.
2 TIMOTHY 3:12

AS A YOUNG MAN IN MINISTRY, I discovered that my grandfather
had quite an extensive Christian library. An eminently godly man, he
desired to fill himself with soul-stirring theology and church history.
One small volume that stood out to me as I rummaged through his
collection after his death was *Foxe's Book of Martyrs*. A paperback with
a purple cover, it had pages dog-eared and tattered from obvious use.
Originally published in 1563, the book chronicled the vivid English
and Scottish accounts of Protestant suffering and martyrdom under
the reign of the Roman Catholic Church. Though its author, John
Foxe, filled the book with illustrations of torment, anguish, and
burning, he fostered within me a love not only for this time period
but also for the persecuted church both throughout church history
and in many places today.

Foxe chronicles the history of a man by the name of John Hooper.
Born in 1495 in Somerset, England, Hooper became bishop of

Gloucester and then bishop of Worcester. His early life was spent at Cambridge and Oxford. He traveled to France and Switzerland, where he befriended Protestant Reformers, who implanted a zeal within him for Reformation in England. After the death of Edward VI, Mary I (eventually known as Bloody Mary) ascended the throne and immediately began to usher England back to Roman Catholicism. Hooper was arrested and imprisoned in the Tower of London. On numerous occasions, he was ushered before assembled councils and commanded to recant his "Protestant heresy." Every time, he refused.

On February 9, 1555, Bishop Hooper was led to his place of execution in Gloucester, tied to a stake, and burned. Chronicling these events, Foxe tells us that as Hooper was escorted to the stake, he implored the people to join him in reciting the Lord's Prayer. Weeping and sobbing washed over the crowd of spectators. When he reached the erected place of his death, an iron hoop was placed around his chest to secure him to the wooden stake. As the kindling was placed around him, he caught two bundles in his hands, kissed them, and put them under his arms. On that cold morning the blustery English wind was so fierce that the flames barely touched him. The bottom half of his body began to burn, but only slightly, while the fire never reached his upper body, except his hair. Foxe describes the scene:

> In the time of which fire, even as at the first flame, he prayed, saying mildly, and not very loud (but as one without pains), "O Jesus, the Son of David, have mercy upon me, and receive my soul!" After the second fire was spent, he did wipe both his eyes with his hands, and beholding the people, he said with an indifferent loud voice, "For God's love, good people, let me have more fire!"[1]

1   John Foxe, *Fox's Book of Martyrs* (Philadelphia: Claxton, 1881), 227.

A third fire was lit. Amid the waning flames, Hooper prayed with a loud voice: "Lord Jesus, have mercy upon me! Lord Jesus, have mercy upon me! Lord Jesus, receive my spirit!" These were his final words that emerged from the flames. Little by little he burned. First one finger, then the next. One arm fell off into the fire, and then the next, until finally he yielded up his spirit. Foxe comments,

> Thus was he three quarters of an hour or more in the fire. Even as a lamb, patiently he abode the extremity thereof, neither moving forwards, backwards, or to any side; but having his nether parts burned, and his bowels fallen out, he died as quickly as a child in his bed, and he now reigneth as a blessed martyr in the joys of heaven, prepared for the faithful in Christ before the foundations of the world, for whose constancy all Christians are bound to praise God.[2]

Countless stories like this can be recited from church history, and even today in certain places around the world, where there is a harsh antagonism for the gospel message of Christ.

The Promise of Persecution

The apostle Paul was deeply persuaded that conflict is inevitable between the church composed of those living righteously and those in the world who revel in their ungodliness. There is an undeniable tension between light and darkness. In contrast to the godlessness of the world that Paul outlines in 2 Timothy 3:1–9, he then writes to Timothy:

> You, however, have followed my teaching, my conduct, my aim in life, my faith, my patience, my love, my steadfastness, my persecutions and sufferings that happened to me at Antioch, at

2   J. C. Ryle, *Light from Old Times* (Moscow, ID: Charles Nolan, 2000), 108.

Iconium, and at Lystra—which persecutions I endured; yet from them all the Lord rescued me. Indeed, all who desire to live a godly life in Christ Jesus will be persecuted. (2 Tim. 3:10–12)

Paul shares with Timothy the experiences of his persecution and suffering endured at Antioch, Iconium, and Lystra. The word "persecutions" is derived from a Greek verb that means "put to flight." Taking his stand before hostile Jewish leaders and pagan worshipers, Paul refused to compromise or cease proclaiming the exclusivity of Christ and the gospel. As a result, he was driven from towns, beaten, imprisoned, whipped, and stoned. This is quite a contrast for Paul, who, before his conversion, had been the greatest persecutor of the Christian church. For example, we read in Acts 9:1–2, "Saul [Paul], still breathing threats and murder against the disciples of the Lord, went to the high priest and asked him for letters to the synagogues at Damascus, so that if he found any belonging to the Way, men or women, he might bring them bound to Jerusalem." Later, before a multitude in Jerusalem, Paul confessed to persecuting the church, arresting men and women, and putting them in prison, even putting them to death (Acts 22:4). But the one who was the persecutor became the persecuted for proclaiming the same message he had so vehemently rejected.

Lest we think the church is immune to or exempt from persecutions and sufferings in our modern age, Paul reminds us that "*all* who desire to live a godly life in Christ Jesus will be persecuted" (2 Tim. 3:12). The reason for such hatred from the world against the church is that those who make up the bride of Christ "desire to live a godly life." Jesus warned his disciples:

If the world hates you, know that it has hated me before it hated you. If you were of the world, the world would love its own; but because you are not of the world, but I chose you out of the world, therefore the world hates you. Remember the word that I said to you: "A servant is not greater than his master." If they persecuted me, they will also persecute you. If they kept my word, they will also keep yours. But all these things they will do to you on account of my name, because they do not know him who sent me. (John 15:18–21)

Every faithful believer must expect persecution. Not that every believer will be tortured, imprisoned, asked to recant, or even burned at a stake—but you will experience, at one point or another, opposition from the world. What does this mean for the church? It means that the church is composed of those whom the world despises. There may be a facade of friendliness and desire for cooperation, but in the recesses of the heart of the ungodly, there is a vehement hatred for the things of God and the good news of the gospel.

Reasons for Persecution

In his concluding beatitude in Matthew 5, Jesus pronounces divine blessing upon those who suffer persecution:

> Blessed are those who are persecuted for righteousness' sake, for theirs is the kingdom of heaven.
> Blessed are you when others revile you and persecute you and utter all kinds of evil against you falsely on my account. (vv. 10–11)

Why will the followers of Christ face persecution? Because their lives are characterized by the previous beatitudes—poverty of spirit, mourning over their sin, meekness, thirst and hunger for righteousness, mercy, purity, and peacemaking. Perhaps this is what Paul had in mind when he wrote to Timothy that those who desire holiness will inevitably face persecution (2 Tim. 3:12).

Within this beatitude, Jesus defines persecution arising from two sources.

First, true disciples of Christ are persecuted "for righteousness" (Matt. 5:10). The Beatitudes are often divided into two groups of four, each group ending with a reference to righteousness. The first group concludes with a response to a kind of spiritual emptiness often present within followers of Christ. It is not that we are lacking salvation but that we now have a new recognition of who we are before God. With supplication and humility before God's majesty (v. 3), grief due to our indwelling sin (v. 4), and a meekness in service to him and others (v. 5), we are always hungry and thirsty for righteousness (v. 6). The succeeding group of beatitudes ends in verse 10 with the type of righteousness that draws persecution. The characteristics that often elicit persecution from the world are mercy (v. 7), purity (v. 8), and peacemaking (v. 9). Jesus makes clear that those who live ungodly lives will condemn the righteousness of those striving to walk in godliness.

Second, true disciples of Christ are persecuted "on my [Jesus's] account," or as several translations put it, "because of me [Jesus]" (v. 11). Later in Matthew's Gospel, Jesus forewarns his followers of the type of treatment they can expect: "You will be hated by all for *my name's sake*" (10:22). Persecution comes to the followers of Christ because of our intimate identification with him as our Savior and Lord. Particularly, in Luke 6:22, Jesus pinpoints a Christological title that often occasions the suffering of his disciples identified with it. The specific title of "Son of Man" instigates hostility from an unbelieving world. This title identifies Jesus as a divine, heavenly King, who reigns over a universal and eternal kingdom. In addition, because of such majestic sovereignty, he alone is ultimately worthy and commands the worship of all the peoples of the earth. For it will be the "Son of Man" who "will send his angels, and they will gather out of his kingdom all causes of sin and all law-breakers" (Matt. 13:41). It is the "Son of Man" who "is going to come with his angels in the glory of his Father," when he "will repay each person according to what he has done" (Matt. 16:27). It is the "Son of Man coming in his kingdom" (Matt. 16:28), the "Son of Man" who "will sit on his glorious throne" (Matt. 19:28). At the end of Jesus's life, while he was on trial before the high priest Caiaphas and the religious leaders, this very title caused him to be labeled blasphemous and therefore worthy of death.

> "I adjure you by the living God, tell us if you are the Christ, the Son of God." Jesus said to him, "You have said so. But I tell you, from now on you will see the Son of Man seated at the right hand of Power and coming on the clouds of heaven." Then the high priest tore his robes and said, "He has uttered blasphemy." (Matt. 26:63–65)

An unbelieving world is agreeable with the church that identifies Jesus as a moral teacher, inspirational role model, or great leader. But the world becomes indignant toward the church when she attributes to Christ divine authority, sovereign kingship, and wor-shipful adoration. When the church identifies with the Christ of the Bible—divine ruler of the cosmos, worthy of all worship—she exhibits an alien righteousness that is unique in character. This righteousness is not of her own making or invention. This distinctive, heavenly righteousness has been gifted to her by Christ on the cross, who desired to beautify his bride by granting her an unparalleled message: Jesus is King.

Expressions of Persecution

Jesus proceeds in Matthew 5:11 to offer three expressions of persecution that his followers will experience in their pilgrimage on earth. First, he says that others will "revile you." Reviling is the picture of someone mocking and verbally shaming you, pronouncing over you humiliating and discrediting words. We all know people in our communities who despise everything we stand for and the message preached every Lord's Day from the pulpits of our local churches. They roam about in the community mocking the church and its members.

Second, the word "persecute" in verse 11 means "run after, pursue, or run out." Jesus is warning his disciples that they may be sought from town to town by those driven by evil intentions, may endure violent abuse, and may even be turned over to the authorities. In Matthew 10, when Jesus warns of the hate his followers will endure because of their identification with him, he says, "When they persecute you in one town, flee to the next" (v. 23). Those who are incensed by the gospel message may seek to drive a pastor out of town. Those who are enraged by the evangelistic efforts of a church may seek to bring that church before the authorities for violating their privacy. All manner of things may be invented to pursue you, run after you, or even run you out of town. The church must be a beacon of gospel light within a community seeking its good by proclaiming the saving message of Jesus Christ. Some will see this as a beautiful representation of the transforming power of Christ, while others will hate this very effort and will seek to persecute Christ's followers.

Third, Matthew 5:11 states that your adversaries will "utter all kinds of evil against you falsely on my account." The persecutors of Jesus's followers will raise allegations against them that have no basis in reality but are lies. The Pharisees said of Jesus, "It is only by Beelzebul, the prince of demons, that this man casts out demons" (Matt. 12:24). They were accusing Jesus of being the pinnacle of evil and of casting out demons in the name of hell. In Acts 24, the high priest Ananias brings formal charges against the apostle Paul, accusing him of being a "plague, one who stirs up riots among all the Jews throughout the world and is a ringleader of the sect of the Nazarenes" (v. 5). There is no substance to deceitful lies, false accusations, and mockery invented to persecute those within the church. A church devoted to righteousness, godliness, and the gospel of Christ will be persecuted and reviled because that same righteousness, godliness, and gospel come as an indictment against the sinful lifestyle of unbelievers. "For everyone who does wicked things hates the light and does not come to the light, lest his works should be exposed" (John 3:20).

It's often the case that the devil, our mutual enemy, thinks he can destroy the church by persecution. However, throughout church history, we learn that persecution is a catalyst for church growth and increase instead of destruction. In Acts, when Luke records that the religious leaders seized the apostles and imprisoned them, he adds, "But many of those who had heard the word believed, and a number of the men came to about five thousand" (Acts 4:4). After Stephen was stoned and at the height of Saul's persecution of the church, her members "scattered throughout the regions" (Acts 8:1), but several new congregations were established as far away as "Phoenicia and Cyprus and Antioch" by the scattered believers (Acts 11:19). The apostle Paul observed a similar gospel advance when he was persecuted:

> I want you to know, brothers, that what has happened to me has really served to advance the gospel, so that it has become known

throughout the whole imperial guard and to all the rest that my imprisonment is for Christ. And most of the brothers, having become confident in the Lord by my imprisonment, are much more bold to speak the word without fear. (Phil. 1:12–14)

Justin Martyr, in his dialogue with Trypho the Jew, wrote that as a result of persecution in his day, the church was fruitful and flourishing:

It is evident that none can terrify or affright and bring under any of us who throughout the whole world believe in Jesus. For while we are under the agonies of death, under the tortures of the cross, are exposed to wild beasts, and punished with bonds and fire and every other kind of torment, it is certain that we do not depart from our profession. But by how much the more we are afflicted with such sort of torments, by so much the more does the number of the faithful and true worshippers of God increase through the name of Jesus. Just as when one prunes off some of the fruitful parts of a vine to make the other branches more flourishing and more fruitful, so it happens with us.[3]

By persecuting the church, the devil deceives himself into thinking he can stop her mission in the world. Persecution serves to display the righteousness, courage, boldness, and power of the gospel of Christ and achieves the very opposite of its purpose. Believers are sanctified, congregations grow, fear departs, the gospel is more boldly proclaimed, unbelievers are saved, and the body of Christ is beautified.

This final beatitude, Matthew 5:11, is a blessing Jesus pronounces over those who identify with him. He is saying of them, in effect,

3   Justin Martyr, *Justin Martyr's Dialogue with Trypho the Jew*, ed. and trans. Henry Brown (London: Macmillan, 1864), 234–36.

"When you are persecuted, reviled, pursued, slandered, ridiculed, beaten, mocked, arrested, murdered—you are mine!"

Rejoice and Be Glad!

If we were only given Matthew 5:11, we might despair. But Jesus gives us more: "Rejoice and be glad, for your reward is great in heaven, for so they persecuted the prophets who were before you" (Matt. 5:12). What a seemingly odd follow-up to what could be a very discouraging pronouncement in verse 11. Jesus is not being insensitive here by dismissing the severity of persecution or the fear that often accompanies it. Rather, the King of glory is looking out over the people, many of whom would face martyrdom, and saying, in essence, "Regardless of what you suffer on my account, I can assure you that the reward I have prepared for you in heaven will far more than compensate for any persecution you have endured here in my name."

There is a paradoxical mystery within the words "Rejoice and be glad, for your reward is great in heaven." Rejoice while suffering? Be glad amid ridicule? How can this be? This mystery is unveiled in the depth of our unyielding assurance that being with Jesus in glory will far more than reward us for any suffering we have faced in this life. Paul reminds the church at Corinth of this glorious truth: "For this light momentary affliction is preparing for us an eternal weight of glory beyond all comparison, as we look not to the things that are seen but to the things that are unseen. For the things that are seen are transient, but the things that are unseen are eternal" (2 Cor. 4:17–18). Our rejoicing and gladness proceed from faith in the unseen realm of eternity. The same faith that accepts Jesus Christ as Lord. The same faith that transforms us from one degree of glory to another. The same faith that stares our persecutors in the face and prays, "Father, forgive them; they do not know what they are doing." These persecutions are "preparing for us" or "bringing about" an "eternal weight of glory." The reward is out of this world, for Jesus is preparing it.

To "be glad" is to enjoy a state of utter happiness and well-being. "Rejoice" is similar in meaning to being glad but is more intense. This denotes extreme gladness and extreme joy.

Both these verbs in the Greek are present tense. Jesus is commanding his followers to be consistently and continually joyful and glad amid suffering and persecution. This divinely gifted joy rejoices as our persecutors hurl lies, hate, and accusations against us. A spring of refreshment amid the darkest hour of suffering, this joy rejoices in Christ despite the pain of persecution. It was the immediate type of joy the apostles expressed in Acts 5:40–41 in the face of their persecution: "And when [the council] had called in the apostles, they beat them and charged them not to speak in the name of Jesus, and let them go. Then they left the presence of the council, *rejoicing* that they were counted worthy to suffer dishonor for the name." With bruises forming, blood dripping from whiplashes, and their garments torn from their bodies, they rejoiced.

Jesus's command to rejoice in the face of persecution leaves no room for the church to stagger into self-pity and dejection. Far too many of us are known more for our whining and complaining than for our rejoicing and gladness. Self-pity spoils the garments of Christ's bride and defaces her beauty. The only acceptable responses to persecution are joy and celebration, with the firm assurance that our treasure resides in heaven, not in this temporal world. Paul shows us that our joy, as believers yet in this world, is always mingled with sorrow. Believers should be "sorrowful, yet always rejoicing" (2 Cor. 6:10). We are sorrowful at the condition of the hearts of our persecutors while rejoicing that we are being persecuted for righteousness' sake.

When we forget to rejoice, we should consider "the prophets" (Matt. 5:12). These prophets are described in Hebrews 11:36–38:

> Others suffered mocking and flogging, and even chains and imprisonment. They were stoned, sawn in two, and killed with the sword. They went about in skins of sheep and goats, destitute, afflicted, mistreated—of whom the world was not worthy—wandering about in deserts and mountains, and in dens and caves of the earth.

We are prone to forget. So read their testimonies, immerse yourselves in their lives, and you'll soon realize that you stand in line with godly men and women of all generations who named the name of Christ and were hated by the world. You are part of that church, the universal church of all the ages proceeding to glory to hear our Lord pronounce, "Well done."

Three weeks before John Hooper was led to the stake of his execution, he wrote the following letter to his friends from prison:

> Ye must now turn all your [thought] from the peril you see, and mark the felicity [joy] that followeth the peril—either victory in this world of your enemies, or else a surrender of this life to inherit the everlasting kingdom. Beware of beholding too much the felicity or misery of this world; for the consideration and too earnest love or fear of either of them draweth from God. . . . There is nothing under God but may be kept, so that God, being above all things we have, be not lost.[4]

If the joy of the church resides in this life only, we are of all people most miserable. Rather, the joy of the church derives from eternal

---

4 J. C. Ryle, *Facts and Men* (London: William Hunt, 1882), 89.

glory, where Christ reigns as he makes us more beautiful. The church must be known as those who are "looking forward to the city that has foundations, whose designer and builder is God" (Heb. 11:10). Only then is she radiantly beautiful before her persecutors.

The forward-looking faith of Moses is an example to us all: "He considered the reproach of Christ greater wealth than the treasures of Egypt, for he was looking to the reward" (Heb. 11:26).

14

We Are One

There is one body.

EPHESIANS 4:4

THE CHURCH IS ONE.

Few believers would respond to this succinct statement with anything but a resounding "Amen!" However, in practice, does the church operate in a way that demonstrates the truth of this statement? Too often the church is a house divided against itself. We've lost the beauty and loveliness that only comes when there is real and abiding oneness.

Oneness among the people of God is a defining characteristic of the church. We don't have to read far into the New Testament until we find Jesus speaking of the oneness of his bride. The content of his high priestly prayer in John 17 abounds with oneness petitions. He prays that believers "may all be one, just as you, Father, are in me, and I in you, that they also may be in us, so that the world may believe that you have sent me" (v. 21). His people's oneness offers a flawless testimony that he is the Son of God. Not only are we to be *one*, but we are to be "*perfectly* one." In verse 23, Jesus prays, "I in them and you in me, that they may become perfectly one, so that the world may know that you sent me and loved them even as you loved me." Proceeding out of the divine Trinitarian oneness—"I in them and you in me"—is the injunction that believers are to mirror such oneness *perfectly*. This perfect oneness is bound up in the Father's expression of love to his Son, and through his Son, to us. Therefore, his people's perfect oneness is also a testimony to the legitimacy of love expressed from the Father both to the Son and to sinful creatures. The unity of his church is a testimony of the gospel.

Without this unity, the world is likely to see the church as a human organization devised by creative ingenuity, not a body of divine origin. Discord plagues man-made institutions—love, peace, harmony, community, and fellowship eventually break down. Jesus is praying that when the world views the church, it will see not a man-made organization but a divine organism born from God. The church's growing *oneness* is what defines the church as having an *otherness*. Why would the world be supernaturally drawn to an institution filled with conflict, cliques, hostility, fighting, and division?

A Divine Oneness

The apostles took this oneness theology seriously and tirelessly appealed to the church that "there be no divisions among you, but that you be united in the same mind and the same judgment" (1 Cor. 1:10). Paul fills his epistles with the overarching theme of unity among the body of Christ.

Ephesians 4 begins with the admonishment to the church "to maintain the unity of the Spirit in the bond of peace" (v. 3). Then, Paul lists unifying themes that must be present within every church if she is to be a reflection of God and a beacon of the gospel:

- "one body"
- "one Spirit"
- "one hope"
- "one Lord"
- "one faith"
- "one baptism"
- "one God and Father" (vv. 4–5)

Paul presents these as part and parcel of a worthy walk (v. 1). These are the characteristics of a church "eager to maintain the unity of the Spirit in the bond of peace" (v. 3). When these features are present, there is unity and peace. When they are not present, that church is not walking worthy of its calling.

One body. Paul bases his whole epistle to the Ephesians upon this oneness. Whatever the color of your skin, whatever language you speak, whatever pedigree you descend from, whatever cultural affiliation you have, the moment you become a believer in the Lord Jesus Christ, you enter *one* family (Eph. 3:15). We tend to think in terms of denominations. Sometimes we can resemble those who said, "I follow Paul," or "I follow Apollos," or "I follow Cephas" (1 Cor. 1:12). While denominations may be beneficial for maintaining doctrinal allegiances or collective mission efforts, if you are in Christ, you are in one family—God's family.

One Spirit. It can be said of all believers that they are "being built together into a dwelling place for God by the Spirit" (Eph. 2:22). There is only one Holy Spirit. Perhaps nothing has so divided the church as our failure to recognize we are collectively the habitation of *one* Spirit. Peering into particular churches, one would almost think there are multiple Spirits who manifest themselves differently depending on the biblical interpretations of individual churches. But here, Paul says that the *one body* has *one Spirit*. The Spirit indwells her, empowers her, teaches her, sanctifies her, and beautifies her. Without the Spirit breathing life into this glorious body, she would remain lifeless and useless. But through his indwelling, the Spirit raises her to be a shining beacon of radiant gospel light in a dark world.

One hope. Through the Spirit, believers have "one hope." Paul identifies the one Spirit as sealing every born-again believer, becoming the "guarantee of our inheritance" (Eph. 1:13–14). The word "guarantee" can also be translated as "earnest" and is from the Greek word *arrabōn*, which is often used to refer to an engagement ring. The one Spirit gives the bride of Christ a "guarantee" (an engagement ring) that serves as proof that we will be ushered into the marriage supper of the Lamb. The body of Christ has one eternal destiny guaranteed by the Spirit. Jesus didn't ascend to heaven to prepare multiple dwelling places based on your creedal alliance or preference. There will be no lines of demarcation between churches, peoples, nations, or classes in heaven. Only *one* body, brought there by *one* Spirit, through *one* hope.

One Lord. Appearing before the religious establishment of Jerusalem, Peter proclaimed, "There is no other name under heaven given among men by which we must be saved" (Acts 4:12). Paul warned the church in Galatia, "If we or an angel from heaven should preach to you a gospel contrary to the one we preached to you, let him be accursed" (Gal. 1:8). There is only *one* Lord, and he does not share glory with another. The *one* Lord—Jesus Christ—is the central message of the church. We don't proclaim multiple ways to God or multiple Lords to worship, and any message that provides room for more than one Lord and Savior is to be "accursed." Only in Christ "the whole fullness of deity dwells bodily" (Col. 2:9).

One faith. In his small epistle Jude, the brother of Jesus, appeals to his readers "to contend for *the* faith" (v. 3). Distinguishing the bride of Christ from all other religions is her shared faith "once for all delivered to the saints" (v. 3). This shared faith is found in the revealed word of God, without which we wouldn't know God or have a message to herald to the world. The *one faith* is the revelation of who God is, what he has accomplished through the work of Jesus Christ, and what his will is for our lives. We may all come from differing backgrounds, but at the end of every debate and intense discussion is our one common faith.

One baptism. This phrase often trips up churches. There are polemical discussions concerning the baptism of the Spirit, the baptism of believers, infant baptism, and so on. What Paul is communicating here is that the expression and public confession of that *one* faith are through water baptism. This baptism is not for the sake of obtaining salvation but for the testimony that salvation has already taken place. This baptism is obedience in motion. It is *one* because we are all baptized only in one name, the Lord Jesus Christ. Paul doesn't have a baptism different from Peter's or John's or yours. There aren't multiple baptisms. Upon hearing that there was only one baptism, the people of Ephesus were "baptized in the name of the Lord Jesus" (Acts 19:5). This is merely an abbreviated reference to the baptism that Jesus commanded when he told his disciples to go into all nations and make disciples, "baptizing them in the name of the Father and of the Son and of the Holy Spirit" (Matt. 28:19). The *one baptism* is a response of obedience that identifies those who belong to the triune God.

One God and Father. Unlike the pagan systems of the world, the one body ascribes praise and glory to only "one God and Father." And just in case there is a shred of doubt in our minds regarding who this one God is, Paul identifies him as the one "who is over all and through all and in all" (Eph. 4:6). I think Paul lists God last to remind us that the superior quality of unity within the church, the unity for which Jesus prayed, mirrors the eternal God, who is unified in three persons—Father, Son, and Holy Spirit. We worship not three gods but one God—three persons in one God, God in three persons. Martyn Lloyd-Jones points out that Paul probably saved this final "one" to demonstrate "that the unity of the church is a manifestation of the perfection of the Godhead."[1] The same Father of our Lord Jesus Christ is our Father. Our Father is the Father of an untold multitude "from every nation, from all tribes and peoples and languages, standing before the throne and before the Lamb . . . crying with a loud voice, 'Salvation belongs to our God who sits on the throne, and to the Lamb!'" (Rev. 7:9–10).

Lloyd-Jones discerns that the unity Paul is designating in Ephesians 4 "is not just a question of friendliness or fellowship." Instead, "it is something . . . which lifts us up into the realm of the blessed Holy Trinity!"[2] Authentic Christian unity, the unity that makes the church beautiful, is bound up in a mutual relationship with the triune God.

God's will for the church is that we are one in order to reflect him, his love, his salvation, and his glory to the lost world. The church is weakest when she is not conscious of maintaining "the unity of the Spirit in the bond of peace" (Eph. 4:3). There is a beauty and loveliness here that isn't present within any worldly organization,

1 D. Martyn Lloyd-Jones, *Christian Unity* (Grand Rapids, MI: Baker, 1998), 49.
2 D. Martyn Lloyd-Jones, *Knowing the Times* (Edinburgh: Banner of Truth, 1990), 134.

institution, or entity. The church is distinctly and categorically different. For she is "one body," animated by "one Spirit," guaranteed "one hope," saved by "one Lord," guided by "one faith," testifying through "one baptism," glorifying "one God and Father."

The Work of Ministry

Paul then admonishes the church leaders to equip those in the body for the "work of ministry" (Eph. 4:12). He isolates the goal of every ministry: "the unity of the faith and of the knowledge of the Son of God, to mature manhood, to the measure of the stature of the fullness of Christ" (Eph. 4:13). Every church ministry should be intended to foster three things: (1) unity of the faith, (2) knowledge of Jesus, and (3) Christian maturity. Paul clarifies that, without unity in the church, a proper understanding of Jesus will not be achieved, nor will Christians grow to the level of maturity possible.

Since unity of the faith is indispensable to the church's ministries, her knowledge of Christ, her maturity in the faith, and her imaging of God to the world, we must consider it a command and duty to preserve and perfect this unity within the church. What are some practical ways individual believers can foster a true unity that manifests itself within the one body?

Unity requires one-anothering. There are fifty-nine "one another" statements in the New Testament that speak directly to what we are to do or how we are to act toward each other. For example:

- "Be at peace with one another" (Mark 9:50).
- "Love one another" (John 13:34).
- "Serve one another" (Gal. 5:13).
- "Forgiving one another" (Eph. 4:32).
- "Admonishing one another" (Col. 3:16).

- "Encourage one another" (1 Thess. 4:18).
- "Do not speak evil against one another" (James 4:11).
- "Show hospitality to one another" (1 Pet. 4:9).

As these samples show, the "one another" statements divert attention from ourselves to others. Others become the focus of our ministry.

The "one another" passages are not suggestions for a successful life but commands for right Christian living. Unity is impossible when we consider ourselves more significant than others. The anthem of disunity is "me, myself, and I." We desire our opinions to be heard, our views considered, and our plans fulfilled. We could go as far as to say that unity requires the obliteration of self. It is the complete denial of self to maintain love, fellowship, and peace within the church. By obeying these injunctions, believers ultimately obey the second great commandment, to love one's neighbor as oneself (Mark 12:31), which puts the gospel of Christ on display as the transformative power it claims to possess. Have you wondered how you can beautify the bride of Christ? "One another" fellow believers.

Unity requires sanctified truthfulness. True unity in the church exists only where her members declare with one harmonious voice, "Your word is truth" (John 17:17). Based on the inerrant and sufficient word of God, sound doctrine is essential for a turning-the-world-upside-down kind of unity. In John 17, Jesus prays that his people would be sanctified in the truth (v. 17). "Sanctify" translates the Greek verb *hagiazō*, meaning "make holy." It involves setting something or someone apart from sin. How are believers to be set apart from sin and made holy? By truth. Jesus says that God's word contains the proper ingredients for holiness: "Your word is truth." Therefore, since Scripture is the means whereby believers are made holy, our churches mustn't be a smorgasbord of varied beliefs and ideas, but must be an exquisitely set table offering the scriptural nourishment that causes growth into the image of Christ. If a church is seemingly unified without sound theology, her unity resides in amusing sentimentality or overt falsehood. True unity consists of sanctified truthfulness that bases every ministry, every sermon, every lesson, every decision upon the word of God, with an abiding desire for holiness.

Unity requires gospel fidelity. Any church that doesn't have a biblical understanding of the gospel cannot be called a true church. Sometimes the church understands the gospel in evangelistic terms only: justification, forgiveness, and salvation. But a truly robust understanding of the gospel also recognizes that sanctification is founded on the bedrock reality of once-for-all justification by grace through faith. You don't set aside the gospel of justification as you move on to spiritual growth. Every believer needs the gospel every day. And unity within the church is a wholehearted commitment to gospel fidelity within her people's everyday lives. From how we teach children to how we train for ministry, we must be committed to the faithfulness, dependability, and transformative effects of the gospel to have lasting results.

The gospel unifies the very culture of the church. If for one moment we imagine that our creativity, entrepreneurship, initiative, or even intellect is the impetus by which Christians grow in Christ, we will be fractured. Authentic unity is fostered by a daily awareness of our need for the life, death, burial, resurrection, and ascension of Jesus. We need the gospel every day because we sin every day (1 John 1:8–2:2). Because we continue to sin, from now until we enter glory, we need an "advocate with the Father, Jesus Christ the righteous" (1 John 2:1). We need the gospel because we're a community of forgiven people who need to forgive each other (Eph. 4:32). As a community of faith, we sometimes wrestle with people who have the same sinful struggles. We need the gospel because of our communion with God (1 John 1:3). From prayer to reading the Bible, from changing dirty diapers to our daily work commute, believers should be in constant communion with God through the gospel. We need the gospel because of our common enemy (1 Pet. 5:8). The devil sows seeds of discord at every turn to disrupt and fracture the unity of Christ's bride. The gospel truth of Christ is our only guard against his deception. Fidelity to the gospel recognizes that we are helpless and Christ is our only source of hope.

———

In no way are these three requirements presented as an exhaustive list. They only scratch the surface of what is required to maintain the unity within the body of Christ. But they are certainly a launching pad without which we never get off the ground.

Why is unity so essential, you ask? Paul answers that question in Ephesians 4:14–16:

> So that we may no longer be children, tossed to and fro by the waves and carried about by every wind of doctrine, by human cunning, by craftiness in deceitful schemes. Rather, speaking the truth in love, we are to grow up in every way into him who is the head, into Christ, from whom the whole body, joined and held together by every joint with which it is equipped, when each part is working properly, makes the body grow so that it builds itself up in love.

Unity is critical because it fosters maturity, doctrinal stability, discernment, a loving vocabulary, Christlike growth, churchwide equipping, and spiritual building.

Our oneness reflects Christ, who beams forth his glory in every sphere of the church to make her increasingly beautiful. May our prayer echo the words of Charles Spurgeon: "Bless this our beloved church: keep them still in unity and earnestness of heart. In all fresh advances that we hope to make, be with us and help us."[3]

3   Charles H. Spurgeon, *The Pastor in Prayer* (London: Elliot Stock, 1893), 143.

Epilogue

The king has brought me into his chambers.

SONG OF SOLOMON 1:4

A KING'S INNER CHAMBERS are the most secluded, private, and heavily guarded rooms within his palace. Here, his bride is welcomed as his peculiar treasure and joy.

This book has essentially served as a visit to the sacred chambers where Christ dwells alone with his church. We have been led into the inner workings of the triune God as he rescues and sanctifies a people and makes them fit for his glory. Here, we are called his friends, his bride, his possession, his children, his house. Here, we can call him our Father, our Friend, our Savior, our Head, our Helper, and our Beautifier. Within these chambers, the church is robed in beauty, arrayed in loveliness, and set upon a path of lifelong adoration, intimate fellowship, selfless service, and gospel proclamation.

The church isn't just about organization, leadership, function, and vision. There's something much more beautiful and lovely to recognize. The church is about people being rescued, redeemed, and renewed. The church is about savoring, rejoicing, and service. The church is about proclaiming, enduring, and walking. The church is about *being* the bride adorned, beautiful, and lovely.

Though we visit these chambers often, one day our king will invite us into his chambers forever. That celebration will be inaugurated with the marriage supper of the Lamb. In Revelation 19:7–9, the exiled apostle John hears the multitudes in heaven praising the Lord at this great marriage feast:

> "Let us rejoice and exult
>   and give him the glory,
> for the marriage of the Lamb has come,
>   and his Bride has made herself ready;
> it was granted her to clothe herself
>   with fine linen, bright and pure"—

for the fine linen is the righteous deeds of the saints.

And the angel said to me, "Write this: Blessed are those who are invited to the marriage supper of the Lamb." And he said to me, "These are the true words of God."

On this day, the bridegroom will consummate all things, and we shall be arrayed in garments white as snow as we enter eternal, unbroken fellowship with the Father, Son, and Holy Spirit. The church is now waiting and watching for our bridegroom's appearance (2 Tim. 4:8).

Perhaps you've picked up this book disheartened with the church. You've become discouraged because her leaders and members have failed you in some way. You're wondering about her purpose in your life. As a church member, you have questions about her relevance in the life of your family. As a pastor, you're worn out, burned out, and weary of the endless demands, headaches, and worries—your joy is waning. After difficult circumstances have drawn us all away from our local congregations for varied reasons, you simply need a refreshing drink from the well of a thoroughly biblical ecclesiology to revitalize you for new ministry, bold exposition, passionate worship, and wholehearted service.

This book was meant for people who find themselves in a million different places, scattered abroad in local churches in every continent of the world, faithfully plodding, praying for a renewed hope and glimpse of the beauty and loveliness of the church.

The King has thrown open the doors.

He welcomes you to enter.

He bids you to gaze upon his bride and proclaim, "Behold, you are beautiful!" (Song 1:15).

General Index

abba, 42
Abraham
  earthly pilgrimage of, 149
  as friend of God, 46
Abrahamic covenant, 46
À Brakel, Wilhelmus, 26–27, 32–33
abuse, 162
affection for the church, 14
"all things," under headship of Christ,
  59
angel, minister as, 104
assembly, 32, 33–34, 57

baptism, 131, 132–35
  beautifies the church, 135
  oneness of, 173
Bavinck, Herman, 109
beautiful worship, 89–90
bishop, 99
body of Christ, 54–56
  discord within, 70, 140
  love within, 68
  oneness of, 171
  see also church
breaking of bread, 139
"breath of God," 82–84
bridegroom, 18, 27–28, 32, 54, 182
bride of Christ, 15–16, 181–83

Bucer, Martin, 101–3
Bunyan, John, 112–13
buttress, 78

calling to ministry, 114–15
Calvin, John
  on baptism, 134
  on church as mother, 87–88
  on the gospel, 126–27
  and pilgrim analogy, 148–49
Christian, synonymous with being
  the church, 35
Christian life
  lived within the framework of the
    church, 151
  as walking, 145–47, 151, 152
Christlikeness, 147, 150, 152, 178
church
  affection for Christ, 25–27
  authority of, 58, 98
  beauty of, 14–15, 17–28
  as bride of Christ, 15–16, 32
  as Christ's "brothers," 32
  as dear, 13–14
  division in, 140
  as dwelling place of God, 29–30,
    36–38
  as gift of God to his Son, 25

God-centered definition of, 33–34
as God's co-laborer, 129
heavenly origin of, 31–32
as mother of believers, 87–88
mutual love within, 141
in mutual relationship with the
    Trinity, 174
not God's plan B, 39
oneness of, 169–79
otherness of, 170
as pillar and buttress of the truth,
    78–79
proclamation of God's word,
    84–85
separation from the world, 84
universal and local terminology for,
    35–36
as witnesses, 121–22
"Church's One Foundation, The"
    (Stone), 77–78
church government, 97
communion, 136
communion with God, 88, 92
coram Deo, 71
corporate worship, 94–95
cross, 52
Cyprian, 87–88

deacons, ministry of, 105–9
death, as consequence of sin, 51–52
desires of the flesh, 152
discipleship, and baptism, 132
discord, 170
Dodge, Mary Mapes, 75
doves, 19–20
dwelling place of God, 39

Edwards, Jonathan
    on beautification, 64–65
    on beauty of God, 23–24
    on bride of Christ, 15–16, 24–25

on faithful ministers, 105
on headship of Christ, 54
on love of Christ, 49–50
on union with Christ, 53
elder, 99
endurance, 17–18
Ethiopian eunuch, 134
Eucharist, 136
evangelism, 121
every tribe and language and people
    and nation, 35, 126
exodus, and breath of God, 82–83

faith, oneness of, 173
faithfulness, 71–72
family of God. *See* household of God
fears, end of, 44
fellowship, 136
Foxe, John, 155–57
friendship, 47
fruit of the Spirit, 66–67

gentleness, 72–73
Gill, John, 18, 20
God
    abiding presence in the church,
        36–37
    beauty of, 21–25
    delights in the church, 37
    dwells among his people, 29–30,
        36–38
    faithfulness of, 72
    as Father, 40–45, 48, 174
    as friend, 40, 46–48
    holiness of, 51
    omnipresence of, 30
godly minister, 104
goodness, 71
Goodwin, Thomas, 74, 112
gospel of God, 122–25
    unifies the church, 177–78

gospel simplicity, 92–94
Great Commission, 121
Gurnall, William, 129

Hans Brinker (Dodge), 75
hatred, 162
head and body, 32
"head of the church," 54–59
Henry, Matthew, 127–28
herald, 115–16, 121, 124
holiness, 65–66
Holy Spirit
    as beautifier of the church, 64–66,
        73
    as guarantee of inheritance, 171
    as Helper, 61–64, 73
    and unity of the church, 171–72
Hooper, John, 155–57, 167
hope, oneness of, 172
hopelessness, 44
household of God, 29–38
humility, 72–73
husband and wife relationship,
    15–16, 58

"I AM," 41
image of Christ, 150
incarnation, 53
interpreter, minister as, 104
invisible church, 36
"I've Found a Friend, O Such a
    Friend" (Small), 48

Jesus Christ
    affection for his bride, 25
    authority of, 55–56, 98
    bears witness to the truth, 79–80
    as bridegroom, 18, 27–28, 32, 182
    death of, 52
    as elder brother, 54
    exaltation of, 63

as head of the church, 54–60
    lordship of, 55
    love for the church, 49–50, 62
    resurrection of, 52
    righteousness of, 19
    as Savior, 50–55
    as servant, 108
    submitted to baptism, 134
    supreme expression of God's
        beauty, 24
joy, 68–69
Justin Martyr, 164

kindness, 70–71
Kuiper, R. B.
    on church as God's co-laborer,
        129
    on church authority, 58
    on organic union with Christ, 55
    on the sacraments, 132

leaders in the church
    as instruments of Christ's head-
        ship, 58
    as servants of Christ, 97–99
lies, 163
Lloyd-Jones, Martyn, 174
loneliness, 45
long-suffering, 70
Lord, oneness of, 172–73
Lord's Supper, 131, 136–42
love, 67–68
    demonstrated in the Lord's Supper,
        140–41
Luther, Martin, on the gospel,
    124–25

Mary, Magnificat of, 51
Mary I, Queen of England, 156
maturity in the faith, 175, 178
mercy, 106

"Mighty Fortress Is Our God, A"
(Luther), 37
Moses
passing glory of, 92
valued reproach of Christ over
wealth of Egypt, 168
Mount Zion, 34–35

Nadab and Abihu, 40
new covenant, Lord's Supper as, 138
Notre-Dame de Paris (cathedral), 78

old covenant, 40
impermanence of, 92
"one another" statements in the New
Testament, 175–76
orphans, 108–9
overseer, 99
Owen, John, 34–35, 89–90, 112
on deacons, 106
on the love of the Father, 42–43

parable of the lost sheep, 52
Passover, 136
pastor, 99
pastoral ministry, 99–105
patience, 70
Paul
on authority of Scripture, 80–83
on baptism, 133–34
on consequences of sin, 51–52
on God as Father, 174
on God-centered definition of the
church, 33–34
on gospel of God, 122–25
on headship of Christ, 58
on the Lord's Supper, 138–39
on one hope, 172
on oneness of the body, 171
pastoral charge to Timothy, 113–15
on persecution, 157–58

on preaching, 115–16, 125–26
on shepherds, 58
on suffering, 165–66
on walking as a metaphor for the
Christian life, 145–47
peace, 68–70
Perkins, William, 104
persecution, 155–68
catalyst for church growth, 163–64
expressions of, 162–65
reasons for, 159–61
rejoicing in, 165–66
Peter, denial of Christ, 142
pilgrimage, 148
Pilgrim's Progress, The (Bunyan),
112–13
Pontius Pilate, 79
prayer, for the lost world, 127–28
preacher, 99
preaching the word, 115–16
pruning, of branches, 66
Puritans, 112, 116
on baptism, 134
as pilgrims, 148
prayers of, 128–29

reconciliation, 141
reflected beauty, 21–25
rejoicing, in persecution, 165–66
remembering, in the Lord's Supper,
137–40
repentance and faith, 133
reprove, 117
rescue from sin, 51–52
reviling, 162

sacraments, 131–32
salvation, and breath of God, 83
Samaritan woman, 90
sanctification, 151
as beatification, 64–65

Satan, deceit of, 76–77
Scripture
    as God-breathed, 80–84
    and worship, 95
self-control, 73
self-exaltation, 43–44
self-examination, in the Lord's
        Supper, 141–42
self-fulfillment, 68
self-giving love, 68
self-pity, 166
servant, deacon as, 108
shepherd, 32, 58, 99
Sibbes, Richard, 45, 112, 149–50
sin, sinfulness of, 117
Small, James G., 48
Song of Solomon, 18–21
Son of Man, 160–61
soul care, 102–3
Spurgeon, Charles Haddon, 13–14,
        57–58, 118–19, 179
Stephen, stoning of, 163
Stone, Samuel J., 77–78

teacher, 100
Trinity, and Christian unity, 170, 174

truth, 76
truthfulness, and unity, 176–77

union with Christ, 60
    and baptism, 133
    in love, 53
    in nature, 53
    as organic, 55
unity. *See* church, oneness of
universal church, 35–36

vine and branches, 32
visible church, 36

walking in newness of life, 134, 144,
        145, 149–53
widows, 108–9
work of ministry, 175
worship, 88–95
    simplicity of, 92–94
wrath of God, 51

Yahweh, 41

Zechariah (father of John the
        Baptist), 51

Scripture Index

Genesis
1:2 66
1:26 82
2:7 82
3 39
3:1 76
3:2–3 76
3:4–5 76
3:8 29
12 148
17:7 46
18:17 46
28:17 94

Exodus
3 41
3:2 29
3:13–15 41
3:15 41
12:1–4 136
13:21–22 29
33:12–23 22
40:34–38 29

Leviticus
10:1–2 40
26:12 39

Deuteronomy
15:11 106

Joshua
24:15 94

1 Samuel
4:21 36

2 Samuel
6:14 124
22:16 82

1 Chronicles
16:8–11 91

2 Chronicles
5:14 22
20:7 46

Nehemiah
9:25 71

Psalms
18:15 83
25:5 50
27:4 22
33:6 83
38:22 50
50:2 22
65:5 50
68:5 108
72:8 127

79:9................51
85:4................51
115:1...............44

Song of Solomon
1.....................18
1:4..................181
1:15................17, 18, 19, 52,
                    183
4:1–7...............21
4:9..................20
5:10................26
5:13................26
5:14................26
5:15................26
5:16................26

Isaiah
1:17................108
6:1–5...............23
11:2................63
11:4................83
28:5................22
41:8................46
49:26...............50
52:7................121, 126
52:10...............126
54:10...............47
56:7................34
59:2................51
64:8................39

Jeremiah
2:21................32
22...................148
23:3................32
31:20...............40–41
31:31–33...........48

Lamentations
3:22–23............71

Ezekiel
43:4................29

Daniel
7:13–14............56

Habakkuk
1:13................51

Zephaniah
3:17................91

Zechariah
2:5..................29, 30

Matthew
book of.............137
1:21................51
3.....................133
3:6..................133
5:3..................160
5:4..................160
5:5..................160
5:6..................160
5:7..................160
5:8..................160
5:9..................160
5:10................160
5:10–11............159
5:11................160, 162, 164,
                    165
5:12................165, 167
5:14................84
5:23–24............141
6.....................40
6:6..................94
6:9..................41
10:22...............84, 160
10:23...............162
10:28...............44
10:32–33...........134

12:24 163
12:46–50 31
13:41 161
16:16–17 32
16:18 32
16:21–23 62
16:27 161
16:28 161
17:1–8 23
18:12 102
19:28 161
20:25–27 109
22:16 79
24:9 84
24:13 84
24:35 79
26:63–65 161
28:18 . . . . 56, 98
28:18–20 . . . . 121, 132
28:19 . . . . 121, 173
28:20 . . . . 98, 121

Mark
book of 137
4:39 69
9:34–35 107
9:50 175
12:31 176
14:23 136
15:37 83

Luke
book of 137
1:47 51
1:74 51
2:11 51
4:16 94
6:22 160
12:12 63
12:32 45
13:3 135

15:1–7 52
15:10 125
16:16 123
22:14–23 136
22:24 142
22:40 142
23:46 83

John
1:4–5 147
1:12–13 31
1:14 . . . . 30, 79
3:3–8 83
3:5–6 66
3:8 66
3:20 163
4 90
4:23 . . . . 87, 91
4:24 90
6:37 15
6:68 81
8:12 84
10:11 26
12:8 106
13:1–13 108
13:34 175
14:6 79
14:16 . . . . 61, 62, 63
14:17 63
14:26 . . . . 62, 63
15 66
15:5 . . . . 32, 58
15:13 47
15:18–21 159
15:26 . . . . 62, 63
16:7 62
16:14 65
16:20–22 69
17 169
17:17 176

17:21 169
17:23 169
18:37 79
18:38 79
20:21 98
20:22 83

Acts
book of 136
1:8 .... 63, 121, 122
1:11 138
2:41 133
2:42 136
2:46 136
2:47 122
4:4 163
4:12 .... 127, 172
5:28 122
5:40–41 166
6:1–6 106
6:2 106
6:3 108
6:5 72
6:7 105
8:1 163
8:12 .... 123, 134
8:39 134
9:1–2 158
9:15 116
10:36 123
11:19 163
13:2–4 63
16:2 80
16:15 31
16:16–17 63
16:30–31 133
17:6 122
19:5 173
20:7 .... 136, 139
20:11 136

20:24 123
20:28 .... 26, 114
20:28–31 99
22:4 158
24:5 163

Romans
1:1 .... 98, 122, 123
1:9 123
3:11 88
3:23 51
3:24–25 26
5:5 64
6:3–4 133
6:4 134
6:23 51
7:24 52
8:9–11 66
8:15 63
8:26 63
8:31 74
8:32 47
10:13 .... 124, 125
10:14 99
10:14–15 125
12:1 68
12:2 84
13:3–4 106
13:8 109
13:13 147
13:14 152
15:16 122
15:30 64
16:1 108

1 Corinthians
book of 137
1:10 170
1:12 171
2:1 116
2:10–13 63

2:10–16............109
4:1 99
4:2 72
4:13................84
10:16 136
10:17 140
10:21 136
11:1 84
11:3 55
11:18 140
11:18–22 140
11:20 ....136, 140
11:21 140
11:23–26 136
11:24 131
11:25 137
11:26 138
11:27–28 141
11:28–29 141
12:28–29 100
13:1–2.............68
13:4................70

2 Corinthians
1:1 98
1:20................70
1:22................63
3:7–11.............92
3:18................139
4:4 24
4:5 116
4:7 ....127, 129
4:17–18............165
5:7 147
6:10................166
10:4................109
10:5................84
11:3................77

Galatians
1:1 ....98, 99

1:8 172
3:14................67
4:4–5 31
5:13................107, 109, 175
5:16................67, 147, 152
5:16–26............150
5:18................67
5:22–23............63, 66, 67
5:23................73
5:25................67
6....................152

Ephesians
book of.............171
1....................33, 34, 144
1–3.................144, 145
1:1 98
1:3 ....30, 33
1:4 ....33, 39
1:5 33
1:6–8 33
1:11................33
1:12................33
1:13................33, 123
1:13–14............172
1:22................59
1:22–23............33, 55
2....................144
2:1 144
2:1–2 146
2:2 80
2:5 144
2:6 ....26, 30
2:8–9 133
2:10................146
2:18–19............93
2:19................144
2:20................145
2:21................144
2:22................144, 171

3:1 146
3:6 145
3:10 145
3:13 146
3:15 171
3:16 146
3:20 44
4 .... 170, 174
4:1 .... 143, 145, 146,
                      153, 171
4:1–6:20 146
4:3 .... 170, 171, 174
4:4 169
4:4–5 171
4:6 174
4:11 99
4:11–12 58
4:12 175
4:13 175
4:14–16 178
4:15 55
4:15–16 27
4:30 63
4:32 .... 175, 178
5:2 147
5:8 147
5:18 108
5:22–27 32
5:23 .... 49, 55, 58
5:25 16
5:27 .... 19, 64
6:14–17 109

Philippians
1:1 98
1:6 117
1:12–14 164
2:7 108
2:19–24 80
3:9 152
3:10–11 152

Colossians
1:1 98
1:10 147
1:13 15
1:15 24
1:18 .... 32, 55
1:27 45
2:6 147
2:9 173
2:19 55
3:12 .... 70, 72
3:16 175
4:2–6 84

1 Thessalonians
1:10 52
4:12 147
4:16–17 139
4:18 176
5:12 99
5:12–13 58

2 Thessalonians
2:6–7 64

1 Timothy
1:1 98
1:11 123
2:5 .... 43, 127
2:7 .... 99, 100, 116
3:2–3 100
3:4–5 100
3:6 100
3:7 100
3:8–13 107
3:11 108
3:15 .... 30, 75, 78
4:16 114
5:17 99
6:11 72

2 Timothy
book of 80, 111
1:1 98

1:2 80
1:6 113
1:11.................... 99, 116
2:1–2 114
2:15.................... 114
2:22.................... 114
3......................... 80
3:1 80
3:1–9 157
3:10–12.............. 158
3:12.................... 155, 158, 160
3:14.................... 114
3:16.................... 80, 81, 116
3:16–17.............. 59
4......................... 113
4:1 .... 114, 115
4:1–5 111
4:2 .... 111, 115, 116,
           117
4:3–4 117
4:3–5 118
4:8 .... 118, 182

Titus
1:1 98
1:7 99
1:9 99

Philemon
1:1 98

Hebrews
1:1–4 79
1:3 24
2:11.................... 32
2:17.................... 53
8:8–10............... 48
8:12.................... 138
9:12.................... 93
9:15.................... 93
10:11 138

10:19–21 93
10:25 94
11 148
11:6.................... 90
11:10 168
11:13 148
11:16 32
11:26 168
11:36–38 167
13:5.................... 45
13:7.................... 58
13:8.................... 73
13:17 58
13:20 32

James
1:27.................... 109
2:23.................... 46
3:1 115
4:11.................... 176

1 Peter
1–2..................... 148
1:8 68
2:2–3 59
2:9 .... 15, 109
2:24.................... 140
4:9 176
5:2 .... 97, 99
5:3 109
5:8 178

2 Peter
1:5–7 73

1 John
1:3 178
1:6 147
1:7 147
1:8–2:2............... 177
2:1 177

2:11................147
2:20................47, 109
4:19................43, 68
5:14................44

Jude
3....................173

Revelation
1:13–16............95
5:8–9 126

5:9 60
7:9–10..............174
7:14................16
19:7................16
19:7–9.............182
19:12 115
21:3–4.............38
22 24
22:16–17 ....25n6
22:17 129

Union

We fuel reformation in churches and lives.

Union Publishing invests in the next generation of leaders with theology that gives them a taste for a deeper knowledge of God. From books to our free online content, we are committed to producing excellent resources that will refresh, transform, and grow believers and their churches.

We want people everywhere to know, love, and enjoy God, glorifying him in everything they do. For this reason, we've collected hundreds of free articles, podcasts, book chapters, and video content for our free online collection. We also produce a fresh stream of written, audio, and video resources to help you to be more fully alive in the truth, goodness, and beauty of Jesus.

If you are hungry for reformational resources that will help you delight in God and grow in Christ, we'd love for you to visit us at unionpublishing.org.

unionpublishing.org

Union Series

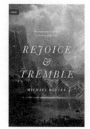

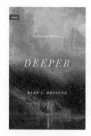

Full & Concise Editions

Rejoice and Tremble | What Does It Mean to Fear the Lord?

Deeper | How Does God Change Us?

The Loveliest Place | Why Should We Love the Local Church?

The Union series invites readers to experience deeper enjoyment of God through four interconnected values: delighting in God, growing in Christ, serving the church, and blessing the world.

For more information, visit **crossway.org**.